With versatile recipes that you can make once and use all throughout the week, Daen Lia is just the ambassador of Mediterranean food we all need right now.

EASY RECIPES FOR EVERY MEAL INCLUDE:

Cheesy Roasted Garlic Bread

One-Pan Roasted Fish Puttanesca

Spinach, Feta & Pine Nut Quiche

Popcorn Eggplant

Crispy Breaded Chicken

Tomato & Garlic Confit Soup with Grilled Cheese

Pan-Fried Steak with Aglio e Olio Sauce

Baked Pasta with Crispy Eggplant & Ricotta

Pan-Fried Salmon with Cherry Tomato Confit

Garlic, Olive Oil + Everything Mediterranean

Garlic, Olive Oil

+

Everything Mediterranean

Daen Lia

PHOTOGRAPHY BY ARMELLE HABIB

SIMON ELEMENT

NEW YORK AMSTERDAM/ANTWERP LONDON TORONTO SYDNEY NEW DELHI

For my mum, nanna, and daughters.
You inspire me every day.

And for my partner, Joel.
You have shown me unconditional
support and love while
I chase my dreams.

Thank you. I love you.

Contents

Introduction

My mother has always said that a delicious meal begins with garlic and olive oil . . .

When my mum cooks, she never follows a recipe. She never measures and she certainly never takes direction. She cooks with her eyes, nose, and heart, making recipes that she has cooked her entire life, which were passed down to her from her mother.

When I was a young girl, Mum's kitchen was a place of chaos, but it's where I found most comfort. It's where I would sit across the bench and tell Mum all about my latest heartache as she sautéed garlic in lots of olive oil for a cozy bowl of her fish soup—it cured any ailment—or watch Mum and Nanna hunched over the stove as they frantically mixed a roux for conclettas, yelling at each other in Italian. It's where I would listen to the sound of pots clattering as Mum forcefully pushed her arm to the back of the pantry to find one large enough to hold her Bolognese sauce.

My mum taught me so much about food and cooking. She showed me the magic that comes from olive oil and garlic, and how just these two ingredients can create something truly delicious.

Garlic and olive oil are at the heart of this book.

Growing up with a Spanish-Italian mum, olive oil ran through our veins and garlic seeped through our pores. We didn't spread butter onto our breakfast toast, we fried the bread in olive oil. Our garlic press was a prized possession that was handed down to my brother, who then handed it down to me. We used olive oil as a seasoning because high-quality extra-virgin olive oil is so luxuriously smooth, rich, and fruity that it rightfully earned a spot next to our salt and pepper shakers.

Food doesn't need to be overcomplicated for it to be nourishing, delicious, or even exciting. Our cooking is simple, unfussy, and calls to be imperfect. It's made to be eaten on the couch in your sweatpants, at a dinner party with mismatched plates, or on the floor with your kids. You might see the mark of your hand in your focaccia, that your puff pastry is thicker in some parts than others, or your fingerprints embedded into your pasta dough.

For years I longed to be that girl who had floral arrangements perfectly matching the folded linen napkins on her dinner table. Or whose homemade pie was shaped into a perfect round. But that just isn't who I am.

My pantry comes with a warning sign, because when you open the door you will probably be hit in the face with a package of pasta holding on for dear life to an overcrowded shelf. My kitchen drawers are surprisingly sparse and are not overflowing with every kitchen gadget you can imagine. I make pasta on my $5 machine from the thrift store that frays the edges of my dough, and I use my olive oil bottle as a meat mallet.

Over time, I have come to embrace these "flaws," even celebrate them. And I encourage you to do the same. If you are using your time and resources to feed your-self and those you care about, then, no matter where it's eaten, how it's made, or what it looks like, your food will always bring comfort and joy. It's indulgent, generous, and made with love (as sentimental as that is to say).

With all of that said, I didn't actually get into cooking until later in life. While I loved to eat and watch my mum, brother, and nanna cook, I always thought of it as their thing. In a previous life, I worked in arts marketing. My career was very exciting and took me all over the world, from Arnhem Land and Cambodia to Dublin and New York. It wasn't until I accepted a marketing role for an arts festival in Tasmania that I found my true love for cooking. Moving to a city where I knew absolutely no one, I was painfully lonely. One of my roommates had a small collection of cookbooks that one day I picked up and could not put down. They were the closest thing I had to friends. I got lost in the words of the wonderful food writer Diana Henry, who described not only the taste and touch of food, but the sounds. I challenged myself to cook all the recipes in these books and would spend every last cent on ingredients for food that I could not keep up with eating. My roommates would always walk in to the most lavish meals awaiting them. From this, a true passion was ignited and the journey of Daen's Kitchen began.

This book is an insight into how I run my home kitchen. It's divided into the core elements that influence all of my cooking: garlic, olive oil, bread, butter, crumbs, and eggs. These are familiar ingredients that I always keep in my kitchen and pantry. And I do mean always. On the very rare occasion that I find myself without olive oil or garlic as I prepare dinner for the family, I am sent into a mild panic attack and my partner, Joel, is sent out the door for a late-night grocery run.

If you were to pull open my freezer, you would find at least a dozen of the recipes in this book tucked away—individually wrapped pieces of crumbed chicken, large plastic containers filled with homemade chicken stock, or ziplock bags holding tomato and basil sauce. A lot of these staple recipes, and many others throughout the book, are the building blocks for either a delicious feast or an entirely different recipe that incorporates them in a small or big way. My crumbed chicken can jazz up your Caesar salad, be used for chicken parm, or be served on its own with roasted potatoes and a simple salad.

For this reason, I offer a lot of recipes that I like to make in large batches. If I am asking you to litter your kitchen floor with breadcrumbs, babysit a pasta sauce for three hours, or get your hands oily slapping and folding focaccia (even though olive oil acts as a great hand moisturizer!), I want it to be worth your while. Because there is no sweeter feeling than unwrapping something from the freezer on a weeknight and thanking your past self for making you dinner.

I hope this book inspires you and that you can turn to it for your next dinner party or cozy night in on the couch. I urge you to cover its pages in oily fingerprints and splatter them with garlicky tomato sauce.

This book is for you, my fellow garlic and olive oil lovers.

Daen

1

Garlic

Garlic confit

Garlic chips

Roasted garlic herb butter

Garlic confit & sour cream puff pastry

Cheesy roasted garlic bread

Crispy smashed potatoes

Garlic confit potato mash bake

Tomato & garlic confit soup with grilled cheese

Clams with garlic, chile & anchovies

Garlic butter–roasted chicken with jammy shallots

Pan-fried steak with aglio e olio sauce

Garlic confit ragu bolognese

Slow-roasted lamb shoulder with garlic confit & anchovy paste

Garlicky brothy beans with parmesan

Lemon & garlic sheet-pan chicken

Garlicky chicken potpie

I find garlic confit to be one of the most beautiful things you can cook. When garlic is slow-cooked in olive oil, something magical happens to it. Its texture becomes soft and velvety, causing it to melt at the slightest touch of a knife, and its flavor becomes mild, buttery, and sweet. It's far less pungent than raw garlic, which is why you will see me use double, if not triple, the quantity in some recipes. Garlic confit is the base of so many recipes in this book because you can use it and its garlic-infused olive oil in anything and everything, from salad dressings and pasta sauces to roasts—and even puff pastry! I encourage you to get creative with your garlic confit by cooking it in different-flavored olive oils, such as chile (page 50) or basil (page 51), using an assortment of herbs and aromatics, or even using an entirely different fat like clarified butter to slow-cook it in.

Garlic confit

Preheat the oven to 250°F.

Separate all the cloves from the garlic heads and place in a heatproof bowl. Cover with boiling water and let sit for 5 minutes, then drain. The skins will become loose and easy to peel off.

Place the peeled garlic cloves, a generous amount of salt, and the aromatics of your choice (if using) in an ovenproof dish and cover with the olive oil. It's important that the garlic is fully submerged in the olive oil so it does not burn.

Roast for 2 hours. There will be a slight bubble to the oil while it cooks.

Allow to cool, then store the garlic with the oil in an airtight container or jar in the fridge for 1–2 weeks.

MAKES 1 HALF-PINT (250 ML) JAR

TIPS

Always make sure your garlic confit cloves are fully submerged in olive oil when storing them. If you are using up the garlic-infused olive oil much quicker than the garlic confit cloves, top up the jar with some extra-virgin olive oil.

Olive oil solidifies in cold temperatures, so I recommend taking your garlic confit out of the fridge at least 20 minutes before you want to use it. Garlic confit should always be stored in the fridge and never at room temperature.

6 garlic heads

Boiling water

Sea salt

Aromatics, such as 4 thyme sprigs or 2 rosemary sprigs, strips of lemon zest from 1 lemon, 1 tablespoon black peppercorns (optional)

3¼ cups (750 ml) extra-virgin olive oil

ALSO USED IN:

Garlic chips are golden, crispy, and absolutely addictive! They make for the most perfect toppings to salads, sandwiches, pizzas, or pastas, adding a much-needed crunchy element. The olive oil is infused with a strong garlic flavor and can be used in all of your cooking.

Garlic chips

Separate all the cloves of the garlic head and place in a heatproof bowl. Cover with boiling water and let sit for 5 minutes, then drain. The skins will become loose and easy to peel off. Using a sharp knife, finely slice the garlic.

Heat the olive oil in an enameled cast-iron Dutch oven over high heat. Place a wooden skewer into the olive oil it, and when bubbles form around the skewer the oil is hot enough. Decrease the heat to medium and cook the garlic for 8 minutes or until it turns golden in color. Move the garlic chips around with a spatula to ensure they do not stick to one another.

Drain the garlic in a sieve set over a bowl, reserving the garlic and its oil separately. Store both in sterilized jars in your pantry for up to 1 month.

MAKES 2 SMALL JARS

1 garlic head
Boiling water
1 cup (240 ml) light olive oil

TIP

Keep a close eye on the garlic when frying it as the chips can overcook at any second!

This garlic butter uses four whole heads of garlic—yes, that's heads not cloves—that have been roasted to caramelized perfection.

Roasted garlic herb butter

Preheat the oven to 400°F.

Using a sharp knife, slice the top off each garlic head, about 1 inch (2.5 cm) down from the top, to expose the raw cloves. Place the heads of garlic onto a large sheet of foil and drizzle with the olive oil. Season with a pinch of salt and pepper, then wrap the heads with the foil. Bake for 1 hour.

Leave the garlic to slightly cool until you are able to handle it. Using your fingers, squeeze the roasted garlic cloves out of their skins.

In a food processor, place the roasted garlic, butter, parsley, parmesan, and a pinch each of salt and pepper. Blitz until all the ingredients are smooth and well combined.

Scoop the butter onto a large piece of parchment paper and roll it into a tight log. Store in the fridge for several weeks.

MAKES 14 OZ–1 LB (400–450 G)

4 garlic heads
2 teaspoons extra-virgin olive oil
Sea salt
Freshly ground black pepper
2 sticks (9 oz/250 g) salted butter, at room temperature, chopped
1 bunch (1½ oz/40 g) of flat-leaf parsley
6 tablespoons (40 g) grated parmesan

Just when you thought puff pastry couldn't get any better, let me introduce you to garlic confit and sour cream puff pastry. With bursts of garlic flavor in every bite, this pastry proves there is no such thing as too much garlic. I must admit, a few years ago I was extremely intimidated by the thought of making homemade puff pastry. It's not something I grew up making, and it terrified me. And while it is a little technical—probably one of the more technical recipes in this book—all you have to do is follow my simple guidelines and you will be whipping up puff pastry like a pro in no time. The possibilities are endless for what you can create with this pastry, which is why I have shown you how to use it in a pie, galette, and quiche.

ALSO USED IN:

- *Mushroom pie with garlic confit & sour cream puff pastry* 95
- *Caramelized onion & goat cheese galette* 99
- *Spinach, feta & pine nut quiche* 160

Garlic confit & sour cream puff pastry

10 tablespoons (5 oz/150 g) salted butter

2 cups plus 6 tablespoons (300 g) all-purpose flour, plus more for dusting

1 teaspoon sea salt

¾ cup (200 g) sour cream

15 Garlic Confit cloves (page 16)

Chill a large bowl, a box grater, and the butter in the freezer for 20 minutes before making the pastry.

Place the flour and salt in the chilled bowl and whisk together. Grate the butter using the chilled grater into the flour. Rub the butter into the flour until you have a pebble-like crumbly texture. You can do this by pinching and rubbing the butter and flour between your fingers.

Create a well in the center of the mixture and add the sour cream and garlic confit cloves. Use a fork to slowly combine the flour by bringing it from the outside into the sour cream and garlic in the center, until most of the flour is moist.

Lightly dust a work surface with flour and shape the dough into a disc. The dough should be firm and moist but not sticky. You want just enough moisture so the dough is barely sticking to itself. If it needs more moisture, slightly wet your hands when working with it or, if it's too wet, lightly dust it with flour. Cover with plastic wrap and leave to rest in the fridge for 2 hours or ideally overnight.

Using a rolling pin, roll the dough out into a long rectangle ¾ inch (2 cm) thick. Fold the dough into thirds as if you were folding a piece of paper to go into an envelope. Turn the dough clockwise and roll it back out into a rectangle ¾ inch (2 cm) thick. Repeat this step six times until you have created many layers and the dough is smooth.

Divide the dough into two halves and wrap each piece in plastic wrap. Let rest in the fridge for a minimum of 15 minutes or up to 2 days before use. If you are not using within 2 days, you can store in the freezer for up to 3 months.

MAKES ABOUT 1 LB 10 OZ (750 G)

TIP

A little trick I learned along the way is to grate very cold butter using a cheese grater. This will make it much easier for you to rub the butter into the flour with your fingertips and evenly distribute the butter through the flour.

This has to be one of the most irresistible dishes I have ever created. No matter what I serve this cheesy roasted garlic bread with, it always steals the show. I might have spent all day making pasta with a slow-cooked sauce, but it will go untouched if this garlic bread is on the dinner table. Not only is it filled to the brim with my delicious roasted garlic herb butter, it's also packed with mozzarella. When baked, the mozzarella melts into the bread and oozes out when pulled apart. If I could categorize it as a main dish, I would. It's addictive. Don't say I didn't warn you!

Cheesy roasted garlic bread

Preheat the oven to 400°F.

Using a sharp knife, cut deep slits into the ciabatta roughly 2 inches (5 cm) apart, ensuring you do not cut all the way through. Spoon 1 tablespoon of the butter and a sprinkling of the mozzarella into each slit. Wrap the ciabatta in foil and place on a baking sheet.

Bake for 15 minutes. Remove the foil and bake for 5 minutes or until golden and crispy on top and the cheese is bubbling away.

Pull the bread apart and serve immediately.

SERVES 4

1 ciabatta loaf
4¼ oz (120 g) Roasted Garlic Herb Butter (page 20)
⅔ cup (75 g) shredded mozzarella

TIP
You can also use my No-Knead Bread (page 127) for this recipe!

These garlic butter smashed potatoes taste exactly like garlic bread, but in potato form. They are buttery, have subtle notes of garlic in every bite, and are crispy and crunchy on the outside while fluffy on the inside. I don't want to boast, but these are the best smashed potatoes you will ever eat.

Crispy smashed potatoes

4 garlic heads

2 tablespoons extra-virgin olive oil, plus more for drizzling

Sea salt

Freshly ground black pepper

3 lb 5 oz (1.5 kg) baby white potatoes, unpeeled

7 tablespoons (3½ oz/100 g) unsalted butter

Handful of finely chopped flat-leaf parsley leaves

Preheat the oven to 400°F.

Using a sharp knife, slice the top off the garlic heads, about 1 inch (2.5 cm) down from the top, to expose the raw cloves. Place the heads on a large sheet of foil and drizzle with some olive oil. Season with a pinch of salt and pepper, then wrap them up in the foil.

Bake for 1 hour.

Allow the garlic to cool slightly until you are able to handle it. Using your fingers, squeeze the roasted garlic cloves out of their skins. Set aside.

Place the potatoes in a large saucepan and cover with heavily salted cold water. (Start your timer as soon as you place the potatoes in the pan on the stove—not when the water begins to boil.) Cook over high heat for 30 minutes or until the potatoes are tender enough for a skewer to be easily poked through the center.

Drain the potatoes in a colander and place in the fridge to allow all the moisture to evaporate. (Alternatively, you can pat them dry with paper towel, but it's extremely important that there be no remaining moisture.)

In an enameled cast-iron Dutch oven over low heat, combine the butter and olive oil and heat until melted. Add the roasted garlic and a pinch of salt and pepper and cook for 2 minutes or until all the ingredients are well combined. Take off the heat and roughly toss the potatoes in the butter sauce. Scoop the potatoes out of the dish, reserving the butter sauce.

Line two baking sheets with parchment paper and evenly distribute the potatoes across them, leaving lots of space around each potato. Wrap the bottom of a water glass with plastic wrap and press it down on the potatoes to squash them a little while still keeping them intact. Depending on your preference, you can smash them quite thinly, which will give you a crispier potato, or smash them only slightly, which will result in a fluffier inside.

Drizzle the potatoes with the reserved butter sauce and bake for 35–40 minutes, until the potatoes are golden and crispy.

Sprinkle with some sea salt flakes and finely chopped parsley and serve immediately.

SERVES 4

TIP

To get that crispy outer layer, don't peel your potatoes as the skin will assist with the crispiness. Also, water is not our friend when it comes to crispy potatoes! I place my boiled potatoes in the fridge for 30 minutes—even overnight—to get rid of every last drop of water before baking them.

This is one of those dishes that leaves everyone speechless. How can you go wrong with silky mashed potatoes with lots of butter and garlic confit whipped through them? To make them even better, after a hefty amount of cheese has been grated on top, the mashed potatoes are popped under the broiler until golden and bubbling.

Garlic confit potato mash bake

Place the potatoes in a large bowl, cover with cold water, and swirl the potatoes around with your hand until the water turns cloudy. Discard of the water and cover again in cold water. Drain the potatoes.

Place the potatoes into a large saucepan and cover with cold water, along with a generous amount of salt (1 tbsp of salt per quart/liter of water). Bring to a boil over high heat, then cook the potatoes for 15 minutes or until soft—a skewer or knife should be able to go through them with no resistance.

Drain the potatoes in a colander and cover with a clean kitchen towel. This will allow the potatoes to steam and remove as much moisture as possible. Allow to sit for 15 minutes.

Mash the garlic confit cloves with a fork and set aside.

Preheat the oven broiler to high.

Over a large saucepan, pass the potatoes through a potato ricer or push through a fine-mesh sieve. In two batches, stir the garlic confit and two-thirds of the butter into the potatoes with a spatula, until smooth and blended. Slowly incorporate the milk until you have a smooth consistency.

Place the potato mash in an ovenproof dish. Scatter the remaining cubes of butter on top and poke them into the mash so only the top is exposed. Sprinkle with the parmesan, then place under the broiler for 7 minutes or until golden on top.

Sprinkle with chives and serve immediately.

SERVES 4

2 lb 4 oz (1 kg) Yukon Gold potatoes, peeled and quartered

Sea salt

40 Garlic Confit cloves (page 16)

10 tablespoons (5 oz/150 g) unsalted butter, cut into small cubes

1 cup (240 ml) whole milk, warmed

2 tablespoons grated parmesan

Finely snipped fresh chives, for serving

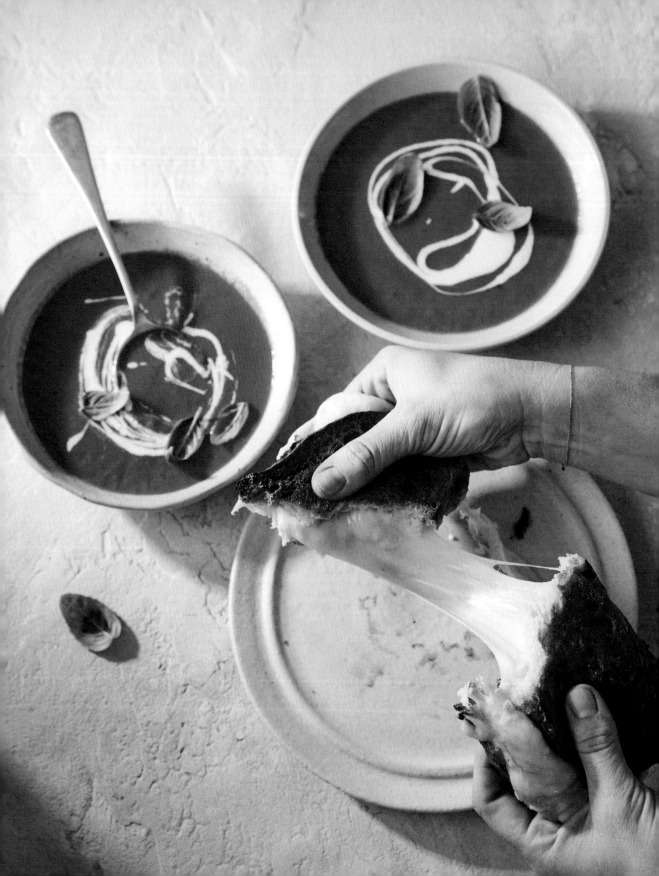

To me, there is nothing more comforting than a big bowl of soup with some carbs on the side. Whenever my partner is sick, he always asks if I can make my tomato soup. I know this recipe calls for a lot of olive oil but it is justified! The olive oil melts into the tomatoes, which are infused with a mild rosemary and garlic flavor. They will be the juiciest and sweetest tomatoes you have ever tasted.

TIP
The reserved olive oil has the most beautiful flavor and works well drizzled over cold dishes, such as salads.

Tomato & garlic confit soup with grilled cheese

2 garlic heads

1¾ lb (800 g) cherry tomatoes

4 shallots, peeled and halved

2 rosemary sprigs

2 cups (500 ml) extra-virgin olive oil

Sea salt

Freshly ground black pepper

1 quart (1 liter) chicken or vegetable broth (page 106 if you want to make your own chicken broth)

2 Roasted Bell Peppers (page 64)

3–7 tablespoons (50–100 ml) heavy cream (optional), for drizzling

Basil leaves (optional), for serving

GRILLED CHEESE

½ cup (125 g) mayonnaise, store-bought or homemade (page 54), plus more for spreading

½ teaspoon onion powder

½ teaspoon garlic powder

2 tablespoons grated parmesan

8 slices No-Knead Bread (page 127) or store-bought sandwich bread

4 slices Gouda cheese

4 slices Swiss cheese

4 slices cheddar cheese

3½ tablespoons (50 g) butter

Preheat the oven to 250°F.

Using a sharp knife, slice the top off the garlic heads, about 1 inch (2.5 cm) down from the top, to expose the raw cloves.

In a large deep baking dish, combine the garlic, tomatoes, shallots, and rosemary sprigs. Cover with the olive oil, then sprinkle all over with salt and pepper. Bake for 2 hours.

Remove the garlic and rosemary sprigs from the dish and set aside until cool enough to handle. Using your fingers, squeeze the roasted garlic cloves out of their skins and remove the rosemary leaves from their stems.

Using a slotted spoon, scoop the tomatoes and shallots into a large sauce-pan, leaving most of the olive oil behind. Reserve the oil in a sterilized jar and store in the pantry or fridge for several weeks (see Tip). Add the garlic, rosemary leaves, broth, roasted bell peppers, and a pinch of salt and black pepper to the pan. Bring to a boil, then turn the heat to low so the soup is at a low simmer. Allow to cook for 20 minutes with the lid off. Using an immersion blender, process the soup until you have a smooth and silky consistency.

While the soup is cooking, make the grilled cheese. In a small bowl, combine the mayonnaise, onion powder, garlic powder, and parmesan.

Spread one slice of bread with a generous amount of plain mayo. Add a slice of Gouda, followed by a slice of Swiss, and then a generous amount of the mayonnaise and parmesan mixture. Finish with a slice of cheddar and a second slice of bread. Repeat for the remaining grilled cheese sandwiches.

Melt the butter in a cast-iron skillet over low heat. Add the grilled cheese sandwiches and cook for 10 minutes on each side, pressing down lightly until golden and crispy and the cheese has melted in the middle.

Ladle the soup into bowls, drizzle with heavy cream (if using), and serve each portion with a grilled cheese sandwich. Scatter a few basil leaves over the soup, if desired.

SERVES 4

The taste and smell of clams instantly transports me back to when my family would go clam digging off the coast of Queensland, Australia. My brother and I would scurry up the beach looking for mounds of sand that indicated to us that a clam was hiding underneath. We would fish them out, throw them into our bucket, then proudly hand them over to our mum and nanna. Back home, Mum and Nanna would let them drain in a colander as they simmered an aromatic base in a large skillet. The house would fill with fragrant smells of garlic, anchovies, and chile. When the sauce was ready, Mum and Nanna would toss the clams into the pan and immediately throw the lid on top. Our eyes were glued to the pan as we eagerly waited for the shells to open. As she opened the lid, my mum would gasp and say, "It smells just like the ocean!" We would gather around the stove and eat the clams straight out of the pan, using their little shells or fresh bread to scoop up the sauce. My hands would always be left so sticky from the sauce!

SERVE WITH:

● *Focaccia* 112

Clams with garlic, chile & anchovies

To remove any grit or sand, place the clams in a bowl, cover with cold salted water, and let them sit for 30 minutes. The water should feel grainy and sandy. Drain the clams in a colander and rinse under cold water.

Add the olive oil, garlic, anchovies, and chile flakes to a large skillet over low heat. When there is a slight sizzle from the pan, cook for 5 minutes, stirring occasionally to ensure the garlic does not brown or burn. Add ½ cup (120 ml) water to the pan and bring to a slight simmer. Cook for 15 minutes or until the water has evaporated and the garlic has softened.

Increase the heat to medium and add the clams to the pan. Stir them into the sauce, then pop the lid on. Steam the clams for 5–7 minutes, to allow their shells to open. Give the pan a little shake from time to time to encourage them to open.

Remove the lid and take the pan off the heat. Sprinkle with the parsley and a squeeze of lemon juice and stir well. Serve immediately, ideally with focaccia to mop up the juices.

SERVES 2–4

1 lb 2 oz–2 lb 4 oz (500 g–1 kg) fresh small clams

½ cup (120 ml) extra-virgin olive oil

6 garlic cloves, minced

4 anchovy fillets

¼ teaspoon chile flakes

Handful of finely chopped flat-leaf parsley leaves

½ lemon

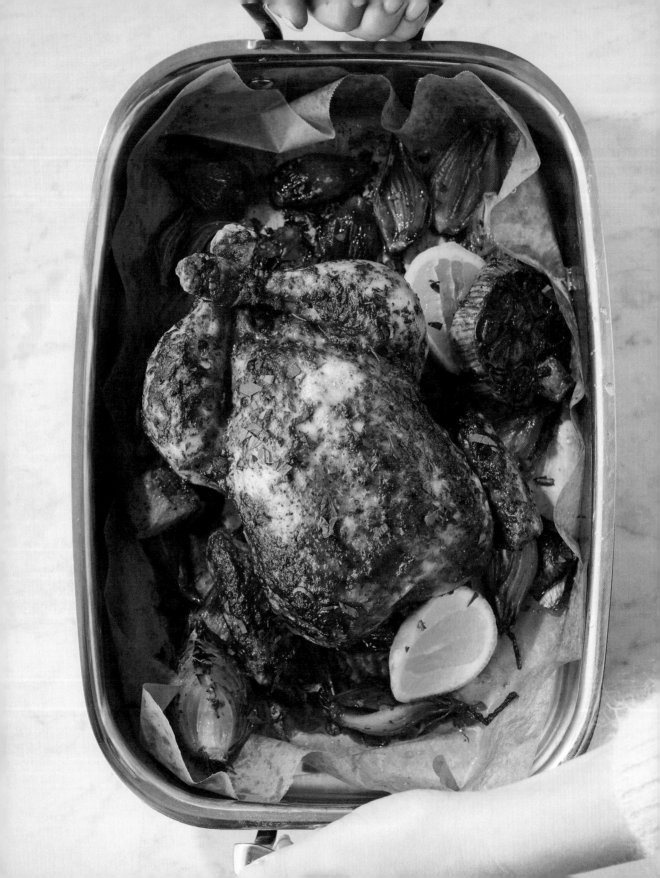

I absolutely adore a roasted chicken dinner—not only because it's so easy to whip up, but because there are so many ways that one dinner can be repurposed. In my house, we usually have one chicken breast left over, which makes the most delicious sandwich for lunch the next day. The chicken carcass will be wrapped up and stored in my freezer, alongside vegetable trimmings to make stock on a slow Sunday morning. Not one inch of this dinner goes to waste! And I mean that literally. When I was testing this chicken recipe, I am not embarrassed to say that I could not stop using my finger to mop up the sauce on the bottom of the dish—it was just so delicious! But what makes this roasted chicken extra special is not only the use of my roasted garlic and herb butter, but also those jammy shallots—sweet, caramelized, and doused in garlic butter.

Garlic butter–roasted chicken with jammy shallots

1 whole chicken
(3 lb 5 oz–4 lb/1.5 kg–1.8 kg)

Sea salt

Freshly ground black pepper

5¼ oz (150 g) Roasted Garlic Herb Butter (page 20), at room temperature

1 teaspoon onion powder

1 teaspoon garlic powder

1 garlic head

½ lemon

¼ bunch of flat-leaf parsley

20 shallots, peeled and halved

¼ cup (60 ml) extra-virgin olive oil

TIP

When storing leftover roasted chicken, keep the drippings and drizzle it over the chicken. This will give it lots of flavor and keep it moist!

Pat the chicken skin dry with paper towels and generously season all over with salt and pepper. Sprinkle salt and pepper inside the cavity of the chicken. If you have time, place the chicken into the fridge uncovered overnight or for a minimum of 2 hours. This step will act as a dry brine for the chicken and leave you with the juiciest meat.

When ready to cook the chicken, take out of the fridge 30–60 minutes prior.

Preheat the oven to 350°F.

Using your fingers, carefully separate the skin from the chicken breast and stuff each side with roughly one-third of the butter. Season the chicken with the onion and garlic powder, then dollop the remaining butter all over the chicken.

Using a sharp knife, slice the top off the garlic head, about 1 inch (2.5 cm) down from the top, to expose the raw cloves. Place the garlic head in the cavity of the chicken, along with the lemon and parsley. Tie the legs of the chicken together with kitchen twine—this will help the chicken cook evenly.

Place the chicken in a roasting pan and scatter the shallots around the chicken. Drizzle the shallots and chicken with the olive oil and season with a pinch of salt and pepper. Bake for 1 hour 20 minutes or until the chicken is golden brown and completely cooked through and the shallots are nice and jammy.

Let the chicken rest for 10 minutes, then carve and serve with my simple salad and focaccia to mop up all those delicious juices.

SERVES 4

My mum's fridge was never without a jar of her aglio e olio sauce. After lightly frying garlic in lots of olive oil, she poured water into the pan, then left it to simmer for 20 minutes. This allowed the garlic to further cook without burning and to become soft and sweet. We would drizzle this sauce on absolutely everything, from roasted vegetables to pasta, but my favorite way to serve it is with a nice piece of steak. I am a rib eye girl through and through, but you can use any cut you desire.

SERVE WITH:

- Crispy smashed potatoes 27
- Simple salad with lemon & honey vinaigrette. 57
- Focaccia 112

Pan-fried steak with aglio e olio sauce

2 boneless rib eye steaks (7–9 oz/200–250 g each), at room temperature

Sea salt

Freshly ground black pepper

1 tablespoon extra-virgin olive oil

3 garlic cloves, smashed and peeled

1½ tablespoons unsalted butter

3 thyme sprigs

2 rosemary sprigs

AGLIO E OLIO SAUCE

½ cup (120 ml) extra-virgin olive oil

6 garlic cloves, crushed to a paste

1 tablespoon capers, drained

½ teaspoon chile flakes (optional)

Bring the steaks to room temperature by taking them out of the fridge at least 30 to 60 minutes before cooking.

For the aglio e olio sauce, add the olive oil, garlic, capers, and chile flakes (if using) to a large skillet over low heat. When there is a slight sizzle from the pan, cook for 5 minutes, stirring occasionally to ensure the garlic does not brown or burn. Add ½ cup (120 ml) water to the pan and bring to a slight simmer. Cook for 15 minutes or until the water has evaporated and the garlic has softened.

Season the steaks well with salt and pepper on both sides and massage the seasoning into the steaks.

Place a cast-iron skillet over high heat. When hot, drizzle the pan with the olive oil. When there is a slight haze coming from the pan, add the steaks and cook for 2–2½ minutes, until you have a golden and caramelized crust. Turn the steaks over and, after 45–60 seconds, add the garlic, butter, thyme, and rosemary and continue to cook for 1 minute. Baste the steaks with the melted butter while they continue to cook.

Transfer the steaks to a cutting board. Drizzle a large spoonful of the hot butter over the steaks and let rest for 5–10 minutes before slicing. Spoon 2–3 tablespoons of the aglio e olio sauce over each steak and serve immediately.

SERVES 2

This is one of those recipes that will always happily feed my family or a crowd. I wanted to share this recipe with the option of using either garlic confit or raw garlic, as it's a great way to show how versatile garlic confit can be and just how quickly you can go through a big batch of it.

SERVE WITH:

🥖 *Cheesy roasted garlic bread* 24
🌶 *Italian-style chile oil* 50

Garlic confit ragu bolognese

RAGU BOLOGNESE

1 lb 2 oz (500 g) ground beef

1 lb 2 oz (500 g) ground pork

9 oz (250 g) ground lamb

Sea salt

Freshly ground black pepper

8 tablespoons (105 ml)
    extra-virgin olive oil

2 white onions, very finely diced

2 carrots, very finely diced

3 celery stalks, very finely diced

20 Garlic Confit cloves (page 16)
    or 6 raw garlic cloves, minced

2 tablespoons tomato paste

¾ cup (180 ml) white wine

1 (24½ oz/700 g) jar
    passata, tomato puree, or
    strained tomatoes

4 tomatoes, peeled and diced

¾ cup full-fat milk

2 dried bay leaves

1 tablespoon brown
    sugar (optional)

1 recipe Tagliatelle (page 164)
    or 1 lb (500 g) dried pasta
    of your choice

Grated Pecorino Romano,
    for serving

Season the meat with salt and pepper on both sides. Roll the meat into large patties in the palm of your hand. Add 3 tablespoons of the olive oil in a large saucepan over high heat. Add the patties of ground beef to the pan and fry for 3 minutes, without disturbing. You want them to be caramelized and browned on one side. Flip and cook for 2 minutes more, until a crust forms on the other side. Break the meat up with a wooden spoon and give it a quick stir. Remove the meat from the pan and transfer to a bowl. Drizzle the pan with 1 tablespoon of the olive oil and repeat with the ground pork. Don't worry if the meat is still a little pink and not cooked through as it will continue to cook once in the sauce. Remove the pork and repeat with the ground lamb. This step ensures we build flavor and texture in the dish.

To the same pan on a medium heat, add the remaining olive oil and bring to the heat. Add the onions, carrots, and celery and cook for 12 minutes or until they have softened and become slightly translucent. Add the garlic confit or fresh garlic to the pan and cook for 3 minutes.

Increase the heat to high and add the tomato paste to the pan. Cook for 3 minutes, stirring quite often, until it turns a deep-red color and is almost sticking to the pan. Deglaze the pan with the white wine and stir for 2 minutes or until 80 percent of the liquid has evaporated.

Add the passata, tomatoes, 1 cup (240 ml) water, milk, the bay leaves, salt and pepper, and the brown sugar (if using) to the pan and stir well. Add the ground meat and all of its delicious juices and give it a stir. Bring the ragu to a boil, then decrease the heat to low and allow to simmer for 3 hours with the lid on, stirring occasionally. Taste the sauce as it cooks to ensure it is seasoned to your liking.

Bring a large saucepan of heavily salted water to a boil. If using fresh pasta, cook for 2 minutes or until very al dente. If using dried pasta, follow the instructions on the package and drain your pasta 2 minutes before the suggested cooking time as it will continue to cook when it's stirred into the sauce. Reserve ½–1 cup (120–240 ml) of the pasta cooking water.

Combine the drained pasta and the reserved pasta water with half to three-quarters of the sauce and stir over low heat for 2 minutes or until you have a smooth and glossy texture. Store leftover sauce in an airtight container in the fridge for 3 days or the freezer for 2 months.

Serve with a sprinkling of Pecorino Romano and my chile oil for drizzling.

SERVES 4–6

I made this lamb shoulder for my partner's family, who loathe anchovies. While I prepped the lamb in my sister-in-law's kitchen the night before, my heart was pounding as I snuck the tin of anchovies out of my bag and onto the kitchen counter. With one eye on my brother- and sister-in-law watching TV across the room, and the other on the tin of anchovies, I very quickly tossed the anchovy fillets into my mortar. It was the perfect crime. Blissfully unaware, everyone absolutely loved my lamb shoulder for Christmas lunch the next day. While it may seem like an odd pairing, anchovies and lamb are a match made in heaven. Anchovies are a wonderful flavor enhancer for lamb as they create a rich and savory saltiness and provide little bursts of umami. When slow-cooked with this lamb, they melt away and it's as if they were never there.

Slow-roasted lamb shoulder with garlic confit & anchovy paste

Preheat the oven to 425°F.

Place the garlic confit cloves, anchovies, oregano, and a generous amount of salt and pepper in a mortar and use the pestle to grind everything together to form a paste. Sprinkle in the lemon zest and rosemary and gently stir them in.

Using a sharp knife, score the fat of the lamb without cutting into the meat. Rub the garlic confit and anchovy paste all over, pushing it down into the slits. Place the lamb in a large enameled cast-iron Dutch oven. Drizzle with the garlic confit olive oil and pour the white wine and lemon juice all over the lamb. Cover the pot with the lid.

Place the lamb in the oven and immediately turn the oven down to 275°F. Cook for 3½–4 hours. The meat is ready when it is tender enough to fall off the bone at the slightest touch.

Once the lamb is cooked, remove it from the Dutch oven and transfer to a serving platter. Let rest for 15 minutes, then shred the meat with a fork.

Serve with my simple salad, olive oil and duck fat–roasted potatoes, and focaccia, or your choice of sides.

SERVES 6

40 Garlic Confit cloves (page 16), plus ¼ cup (60 ml) of the oil

6 anchovy fillets

1 teaspoon dried oregano

Sea salt

Freshly ground black pepper

Grated zest and juice of 1 lemon

2 rosemary sprigs, leaves picked and finely chopped

1 bone-in lamb shoulder (5½ lb/2.5 kg), at room temperature

1 cup (240 ml) white wine

TIP

If you don't have a large enough Dutch oven, make sure you tightly cover the lamb with foil when cooking. The steam will help create that tender, fall-off-the-bone meat.

In my twenties, I had a strong love affair with beans. They are such an affordable and versatile protein to cook with, and they would always leave me feeling full and nourished. When I met my fiancé, beans fell out of my cooking rotation due to his strong distaste for them. He simply cannot stand them! However, after eight years of being together, beans have slowly crept back into my life, and I could not be happier. My favorite way to cook them is in a delicious garlicky broth that's been flavored with spices and herbs. While I haven't quite converted my partner into the bean-lover that I am, this dish may just be the one to change that. It's just that good!

SERVE WITH

● *Focaccia 112*

Garlicky brothy beans with parmesan

2 tablespoons olive oil

1½ tablespoons salted butter

1 yellow onion, finely diced

6 garlic cloves, finely diced, or 15 garlic confit cloves

7 oz (200 g) lacinato kale, stemmed and torn (3 cups)

1 tablespoon sweet paprika

1 teaspoon grated lemon zest

2 cups (480 ml) chicken stock

1 (15-oz/425 g) can cannellini beans

Sea salt

Freshly ground black pepper

2 tablespoons lemon juice

1¾ oz (50 g) parmesan, shaved

Toasted bread or Focaccia (page 112), for serving

In a deep saucepan, combine the olive oil and butter over medium heat. Once slightly foaming, add the onion, garlic, and kale. Cook for 5 minutes or until fragrant and translucent, stirring often to ensure the garlic and onion do not burn.

Add the sweet paprika and lemon zest to the pan and stir for 1 minute.

Add the chicken stock and beans and bring to a boil over high heat. Decrease the heat and simmer for 8–10 minutes, until the stock has slightly reduced and thickened. Season with salt and pepper and stir in the lemon juice.

Sprinkle with the shaved parmesan. Serve with toasted bread or focaccia.

SERVES 4

Sheet-pan dinners were not something that I was very familiar with in Australia. But they seem to be a well-loved dinner option in the U.S., and after being introduced to them and experimenting with them myself, I can see why! They are incredibly easy to throw together, extremely versatile, and are one of the most fuss-free dinners you could make. I truly love a dinner where only a few dishes are required to clean. And this recipe requires minimal ingredients but delivers maximum flavor. It also uses my favorite cut of meat: bone-in, skin-on chicken thighs, which, for some reason, are incredibly hard to find in Australia and tend to require a visit to the butcher—something I will never understand as the chicken skin is the best part, especially when we make them extra crispy like we do in this recipe.

Lemon & garlic sheet-pan chicken

In a large bowl, whisk together the lemon zest, lemon juice, olive oil, garlic, oregano, and a generous amount of salt and pepper until well combined. Add the chicken to the bowl and coat it in the marinade. Cover and let marinate for 1 hour at room temperature or overnight in the fridge.

Preheat the oven to 425°F.

Scatter the potatoes onto a sheet pan and create space in between them to place the chicken. Place the chicken onto the sheet pan skin side up. Drizzle the marinade over the potatoes and chicken. Drizzle a little extra olive oil and sprinkle salt over the potatoes.

Roast for 20–30 minutes, depending on the size of the chicken thighs. Toss the potatoes halfway through cooking. If the potatoes need a little extra time in the oven, remove the chicken thighs and continue to cook the potatoes until golden and crispy. Return the chicken thighs to the pan.

Sprinkle the feta all over the chicken and potatoes along with some parsley to serve.

SERVES 6

Grated zest and juice
of 1 large lemon

⅓ cup (80 ml) extra-virgin olive oil,
plus more for drizzling

2 garlic cloves, finely sliced

1 tablespoon dried oregano

Sea salt

Freshly ground black pepper

2 lb 4 oz (1 kg) bone-in,
skin-on chicken thighs

2 lb 4 oz (1 kg) small Yukon
Gold potatoes, quartered

3½ oz (100 g) feta, crumbled

Finely chopped flat-leaf parsley

I love any recipe that calls for leftover roast chicken, and this garlicky chicken potpie just happens to be one of them. Whenever I make my olive oil–roasted chicken, I always reserve part of the chicken meat to use in my potpie. It's two dinners for the price of one!

Garlicky chicken potpie

2 garlic heads

2 tablespoons extra-
    virgin olive oil, plus
    2 teaspoons for drizzling

Sea salt

Freshly ground black pepper

4 tablespoons (60 g) salted butter

2 carrots, diced

2 celery stalks, diced

1 yellow onion, diced

7 oz (200 g) mushrooms,
    finely diced

½ cup (65 g) all-purpose flour

1 cup (240 ml) white wine

1½ cups (360 ml) chicken stock

2 thyme sprigs, leaves picked

½ cup (50 g) grated parmesan

½ cup (120 ml) heavy cream

1 lb 5 oz (600 g) Olive Oil–Roasted
    Chicken (page 88), shredded

1½ cups (30 g) flat-leaf parsley
    leaves, finely chopped

½ portion (375 g) Garlic
    Confit & Sour Cream
    Puff Pastry (page 23)

1 egg, whisked

1 teaspoon sesame
    seeds (optional)

Preheat the oven to 400°F.

Using a sharp knife, slice the top off the garlic heads, about 1 inch (2.5 cm) down from the top, to expose the raw cloves. Place the heads on a large sheet of foil and drizzle with 2 teaspoons olive oil. Season with a pinch of salt and pepper, then wrap them up in the foil. Bake for 1 hour.

Let the garlic cool slightly until you are able to handle it. Using your fingers, squeeze the roasted garlic cloves out of their skins. Set aside.

In a large pot or Dutch oven, combine the 2 tablespoons olive oil and the butter over medium to high heat. Once the butter has melted and is foaming, add the carrots, celery, onion, and mushrooms. Cook for 8–10 minutes, until soft and slightly caramelized.

Add the flour and garlic to the pot and stir for 1 minute. Add the white wine and stir until all of the flour is incorporated. Stir in the chicken stock, thyme leaves, parmesan, heavy cream, and a generous amount of salt and pepper. Bring to a gentle boil and simmer uncovered for 10 minutes or until the pie filling has reduced and is quite thick.

Stir in the chicken and parsley and cook for an additional 2 minutes. Remove from the heat and allow to cool in the fridge for 30 minutes.

While the pie filling is cooling, prepare the puff pastry. On a lightly floured work surface, roll out the puff pastry into a round that is 12 inches (30 cm) across. Set aside.

Preheat the oven to 350°F.

Transfer the pie filling to a deep round baking dish about 10 inches (26 cm) across. Place the rolled-out sheet of puff pastry over the dish, ensuring the edges are overhanging the sides. Clean up the edges of the dough by cutting off the uneven bits; however, be very careful to leave at least ¾–1½ inches (2–4 cm) of overhanging pastry. Fold the overhanging pastry back over the dish and crimp it with your fingers. Brush the pastry with the egg and sprinkle with the sesame seeds (if using).

Bake for 30–35 minutes, until the pastry is golden and crispy.

Serve immediately.

SERVES 8

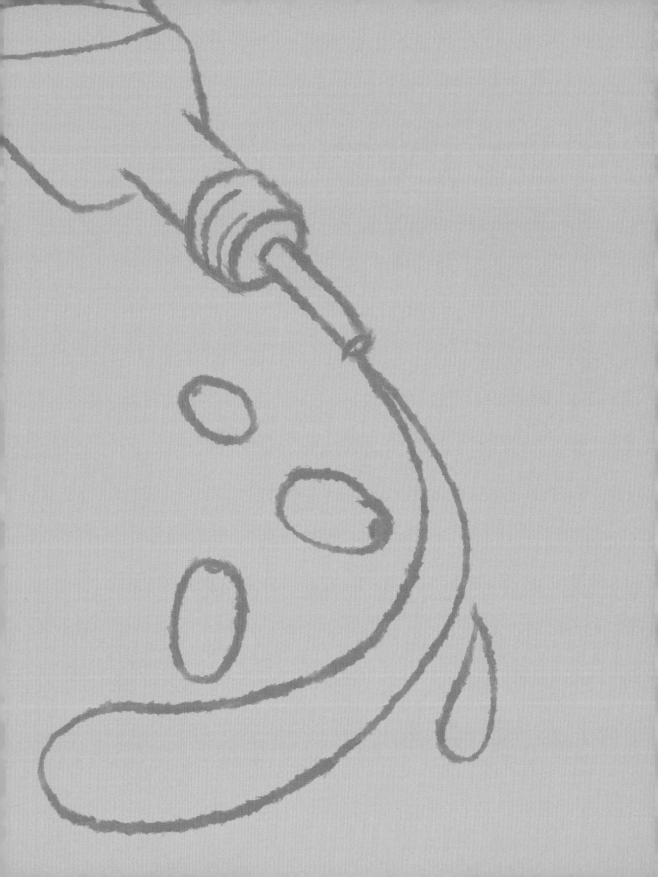

2
Olive oil

We are a chile household. We love to spice up any meal with this Italian-style chile oil, from pastas and pizzas to salads and sandwiches. The chiles are soaked in vinegar for 24 hours as this preserves them and prevents them from going bad and moldy when stored in the pantry. Depending on how much heat you can handle, pack your jars with as many chiles as you like—just ensure they are fully submerged in high-quality extra-virgin olive oil.

Italian-style chile oil

Place the chiles in a nonreactive (glass or ceramic) bowl. Sprinkle with the salt, then pour in the vinegar so the chiles are fully submerged. Cover and let sit on the countertop at room temperature for a minimum of 8 hours and up to 24 hours.

Drain the chiles and rinse very well under cold water. Depending on how you like your chile oil, you can either leave the chiles as they are or finely chop them in a food processor.

Transfer the chiles to sterilized half-pint jars. For a mild chile oil, only use 1 tablespoon of chile per jar. For a spicy chile oil, fill the jar with as many chiles as you can. Fully submerge the chiles in olive oil. Let rest in a cool dark place for 3 weeks, giving the jars a shake once a week.

Store in the pantry or fridge for up to 6 months.

MAKES 3 HALF-PINTS (750 ML)

10½ oz (300 g) fresh chiles, such as bird's eye and large red and green chiles, cut into large pieces

1 tablespoon fine sea salt

3¼ cups (750 ml) distilled white vinegar

Extra-virgin olive oil

TIP

As this makes a large batch of chile oil, I like to gift jars of it to friends and family.

*There is something extremely aesthetically pleasing about basil olive oil.
While it offers a lovely mild herb flavor, it also has a stunning vibrant-green
color that will make any dish it is drizzled over look almost too pretty to eat.
A piece of split-open burrata, spread over bright-red heirloom tomatoes,
acts as the perfect canvas for basil olive oil—especially when glistening in
the sun on a summer lunch table.*

Basil olive oil

Bring a pot of water to a boil over high heat. Once boiling, turn off the heat
and blanch the basil leaves in the hot water for 10 seconds to set the color.
(Do not leave them in the water for much longer than that or they will brown.)
Using a slotted spoon, transfer the blanched basil leaves into a bowl of icy
cold water. Leave to sit for several minutes or until cool, then transfer to
paper towels.

Squeeze as much moisture out of the basil leaves as possible. Place the
basil leaves in a food processor with the cold olive oil and blitz until well
combined.

Line a fine-mesh sieve with cheesecloth and set it over a bowl. Pour the basil
olive oil into the cheesecloth and allow to sit for 30 minutes or until all of
the oil has passed through into the bowl. You will be left with a bright-green
olive oil. Discard the basil.

Store in a dark spot in the pantry for up to 1 month.

1 bunch of basil (about
2¼ oz/60 g), leaves picked

Ice water

1¾ cups (420 ml) light extra-virgin
olive oil, chilled in the fridge

MAKES 1¾ CUPS (420 ML)

TIP

**Use a light olive oil or one that has
more of a neutral color to achieve
that vibrant green color in your
basil olive oil.**

I am quite the tomato snob. I like my tomatoes plump, sweet, and juicy, and will travel far and wide or spend a mini fortune just to get my hands on good ones. I always shed a tear or two when summer and the tomato season are over. However, tomato confit is the best way to preserve summer in a jar. I always make a large batch of tomato confit when tomatoes are at their peak ripeness. They are slow-cooked to perfection in lots of olive oil, with a pinch of sea salt and a sprig or two of rosemary, ready to burst open at the slightest touch. Whenever I have tomato confit in my fridge, I find myself using it as a marinara sauce or as a replacement for canned tomatoes.

Cherry tomato confit

Preheat the oven to 250°F.

Place the cherry tomatoes and rosemary in a large ovenproof dish. Sprinkle with salt, then pour the olive oil over to cover.

Bake for 2 hours. The olive oil should have a very slight bubble to it while the tomatoes cook.

Allow to cool, then store the tomatoes and oil in an airtight container or jar in the fridge for up to 6 weeks.

MAKES 1 QUART (1 LITER)

1 lb 2 oz–1 lb 5 oz (500–600 g) cherry tomatoes

3 rosemary sprigs (optional)

Sea salt

2 cups (480 ml) extra-virgin olive oil

TIPS

The olive oil will have a slight tomato flavor and works perfectly in salad dressings!

Store the tomato confit for up to 6 weeks (or even longer).

Olive oil solidifies in cold temperatures, so I recommend taking your cherry tomato confit out of the fridge at least 20 minutes before you want to use it.

You will also notice that the tomato juices will sink to the bottom of the oil. This is perfectly fine, but these juices do have a high water content, so do not use this part for cooking at high temperatures.

Mayonnaise is incredibly easy to make. All you need is oil, an egg, lemon juice, mustard, and an immersion blender or strong arm. That's all there is to it. When I shared a video on how to make mayonnaise, the internet was sent into mayhem. People couldn't quite believe mayonnaise was 80 percent oil and contained a raw egg. The news broke major media and news outlets with headlines reading, "The internet found out how mayonnaise is made and it is not happy." While I would love to take credit for inventing mayonnaise, it is a French condiment that has been around for centuries, so you can only imagine how stunned and shocked I was to see how unhappy people were with the truth. The sad fact is we have become so far removed from how real food is made that when it's shown to us step-by-step, we can't quite believe our eyes. While most mayonnaise recipes call for a neutral oil, it should come as no surprise that I like to use olive oil. I recommend using a light extra-virgin olive oil, or even half olive oil and half neutral oil, such as grapeseed or avocado, for a mild flavor.

ALSO USED IN:

- Tomato & garlic confit soup with grilled cheese....................31
- Steak sandwich with roasted garlic herb butter, green herb sauce & fries 119
- Leftover roasted chicken sandwich 119
- Creamy egg salad..............163

Olive oil mayo

Place the egg yolk, mustard, lemon juice, salt, and oil in a tall glass container or jug that is just wide enough to fit an immersion blender. Using the immersion blender, process the ingredients together, being careful to not move the blender up and down. Once the ingredients begin to emulsify, start to move the blender up and down while slowly incorporating all of the oil. Continue until you have a thick consistency.

Store in an airtight container or jar in the fridge for up to 3 days.

MAKES 1 CUP (240 ML)

1 egg yolk

1 teaspoon Dijon mustard

2 teaspoons lemon juice

Pinch of sea salt

½ cup (120 ml) light olive oil

½ cup (120 ml) grapeseed oil

TIP

For a mild garlic flavor, use the reserved olive oil from the Garlic Confit (page 16).

My mum and I like to call this our master sauce. We use it in so many of our recipes that my fridge or freezer is never without a batch. You will see it pop up in my baked pasta, bread-stuffed eggplant, popcorn eggplant, and chicken parm. It's an extremely simple sauce, but sometimes simple is best. Simple will give you a delicious and flexible base to work with for other recipes.

ALSO USED IN:

🌿 *Rosemarys
(bread-stuffed eggplants)* *67*

🌿 *Baked pasta with
crispy eggplant & ricotta* *71*

🍆 *Popcorn eggplant* *135*

🍆 *Chicken parm* *146*

Tomato & basil sauce

⅓ cup (80 ml) extra-virgin olive oil

4 garlic cloves, peeled but whole

1 onion, peeled and halved

4 (14.5-oz/400 g) cans
    diced tomatoes

1 parmesan rind (optional)

1 bunch of basil (2 oz/55 g),
    leaves picked

1 tablespoon brown sugar

Sea salt

Freshly ground black pepper

Place the olive oil, garlic, and onion in a large saucepan over medium heat. Cook for 2–3 minutes, until the garlic is turning a very light golden color. Add the canned tomatoes, parmesan rind (if using), three-quarters of the basil leaves, the brown sugar, and a generous amount of salt and pepper. Stir until well combined and bring to a simmer. Once simmering, turn the heat to low and cook for 30 minutes, stirring occasionally.

Using a slotted spoon, scoop out the garlic cloves, parmesan rind, and onion and discard. Scatter the remaining basil leaves on top and serve the sauce on its own with pasta or with the suggested recipes above. You can also store the sauce in sterilized jars, plastic containers, or ziplock bags in the fridge for up to 3 days or in the freezer for 3 months.

MAKES ABOUT 2 QUARTS (3¾ LB/1.75 KG)

When it comes to salad, I only recently learned that the way you cut your vegetables, cheese, or even your lettuce will entirely change the way a salad tastes. Using a vegetable peeler to slice your cheese is a total game changer as it will result in the most perfect little slivers of saltiness. Who knew vegetable peelers weren't just for vegetables? At first glance this salad may look boring. However, when you're eating a succulent, fatty piece of slow-cooked lamb or a fried piece of crumbed chicken, this zesty and light salad is exactly what my indulgent, rich, and generous recipes are screaming out for. This salad is on constant rotation in our house, which is why I like to make the dressing in a large batch to store in the fridge.

Simple salad with lemon & honey vinaigrette

3½ oz (100 g) salad greens, such as arugula, field greens, kale, radicchio, or oak leaf lettuce

Lemon & Honey Vinaigrette (recipe follows)

¼ red onion, thinly sliced

1¾ oz (50 g) Pecorino Romano, finely shaved

Place the salad greens in a large bowl. Drizzle 2–5 tablespoons (30–75 ml) of the dressing over the top and massage it into the leaves with your hands. Sprinkle the red onion and Pecorino Romano over the top and serve immediately.

SERVES 4

Lemon & honey vinaigrette

1 cup (240 ml) extra-virgin olive oil

⅓ cup (80 ml) lemon juice

2 tablespoons honey

Grated zest of 2 lemons

1 heaping teaspoon Dijon mustard

2 garlic cloves, thinly sliced

Sea salt

Freshly ground black pepper

Place all of the ingredients in a large jar with a lid and shake well until combined. Store in the fridge for several weeks.

MAKES 1¼ CUPS (300 ML)

TIP

I like to use the reserved olive oil from my Cherry Tomato Confit (page 52) for this dressing as it adds a lovely roasted tomato flavor.

In my quest to create the world's best roasted potatoes (I take my roasted potatoes very seriously), I have learned a few things: (1) Parboil the potatoes. Not only will this slightly cook them and help with that crispy outer layer, it's also a great way to save on time. You can keep parboiled potatoes in the fridge for several days before you are ready to roast them; (2) Rough the parboiled potatoes up with a spoon to create more surface area and, thus, more crispiness; (3) Steam-dry the potatoes by draining them in a colander, then letting them sit covered with a kitchen towel, to remove as much moisture as possible; (4) Get your fats piping hot. Pop a baking dish with the duck fat and olive oil into a preheated oven and allow it to get really hot.

Olive oil & duck fat–roasted potatoes

Preheat the oven to 400°F.

Cut the potatoes in half lengthwise, then cut the halved potatoes into thirds or quite large chunks.

Place the potatoes into a large bowl, cover with cold water, and swirl the potatoes around with your hand until the water turns cloudy. Discard of the water and cover again in cold water. Drain the potatoes.

Place the potatoes in a large saucepan, cover with cold water, and add a generous amount of fine sea salt (roughly 1 tablespoon for every liter of water). Add the rosemary, thyme, and garlic cloves. Place the pan over high heat and wait for the water to boil. Once boiling, cook the potatoes for 7 minutes, or until fork-tender.

Drain the potatoes in a colander and discard the garlic cloves and herbs. Rough up the potatoes by mixing them with a spoon or roughly shaking them in the colander to increase the surface texture. Cover the colander with a clean kitchen towel and let the potatoes steam for 15 minutes.

While the potatoes are steaming, add the duck fat and olive oil to a baking dish and place it in the oven until piping hot, about 10 minutes.

Very carefully, pour the potatoes into the baking dish with the hot fats—you will hear a delightful sizzling sound. Stir the potatoes into the hot fats, then bake for 45 minutes, tossing and basting with the olive oil and duck fat every 15 minutes.

Remove the potatoes from the baking dish and serve with a sprinkling of grated Pecorino Romano and flaky sea salt.

SERVES 4

2 lb 4 oz (1 kg) Yukon Gold potatoes, peeled

Sea salt

4 rosemary sprigs

4 thyme sprigs

6 garlic cloves, peeled but whole

⅓ cup (70 g) duck fat

⅓ cup (80 ml) extra-virgin olive oil

Freshly grated Pecorino Romano, for serving

Flaky sea salt, for serving

During the summer stone-fruit season, I have a problem. I am utterly addicted to eating peaches—especially when they are lightly grilled with a touch of sea salt flakes and pepper and a drizzle of olive oil. Peaches are yearning to be served in savory dishes. I would be so bold as to say that they are more savory than sweet. With their tart, floral, and delicate flavor, they like to be paired with juicy tomatoes, creamy burrata, and slightly pickled red onions—perfection in a bowl! For some reason, whenever I share my love for peaches in savory dishes, it tends to be rather polarizing. While some people get it, others are outraged to see a peach treated the same way as a vegetable. If you are on the other side of the fence from me, just trust me on this one. Once you begin to cook with peaches the way I do, you will understand what I have been talking about. Join the savory peach movement and you will never look back!

SERVE WITH:

Whole roasted snapper with green anchovy butter 105

Grilled peach, tomato & burrata salad with basil olive oil

2 large peaches, cut into 1½-inch (4 cm) wedges

Sea salt

Freshly ground black pepper

1 tablespoon extra-virgin olive oil

3 Roma tomatoes, cut into wedges 1½ inches (4 cm) thick

¼ red onion, thinly sliced

2 tablespoons Basil Olive Oil (page 51), plus more for drizzling

2 teaspoons red wine vinegar

1 (4½ oz/125 g) ball burrata

Handful of flat-leaf parsley leaves, chopped

Place the peach wedges in a large bowl. Season with a pinch of salt and pepper and drizzle with the plain extra-virgin olive oil. Mix to combine.

In a grill pan over high heat, cook the peach wedges for 1–2 minutes on each side, until grill marks appear. Transfer to a large bowl and allow to cool slightly.

Add the tomatoes, onion, basil olive oil, and vinegar to the peaches. Season generously with salt and pepper, gently stir to combine, and allow the salad to sit for 5–10 minutes before serving.

Push the salad to the side and place the burrata in the bowl. Cut the burrata open and drizzle the salad with more basil olive oil. Sprinkle the parsley over the top of the salad, then serve.

SERVES 4

When I was younger, I was absolutely obsessed with olives. I had no self-control when eating them. This olive confit with whipped ricotta and cream cheese has to be one of my favorite ways to eat olives. They are tender, softer in flavor, and pure bliss when eaten warm out of the oven. The only downside is having to share them with my two-year-old fellow olive-loving daughter. As they say: like mother like daughter.

ALSO USED IN:

✂ *One-pan crispy chicken thighs with caramelized onions & lemon.....80*

⬤ *Focaccia........................112*

Olive confit with whipped ricotta & cream cheese

To make the olive confit, preheat the oven to 250°F.

Separate all the cloves from the garlic head and place them in a heatproof bowl. Cover with boiling water and let sit for 5 minutes, then drain. The skins will become loose and easy to peel off.

Drain the olives, reserving the brine. (Store the olive brine in a glass jar in the fridge to use in my crispy chicken on page 80.)

Place all the confit ingredients in a large, deep ceramic baking dish. Bake for 2 hours. The oil should be bubbling slightly while cooking.

Remove from the oven and let cool slightly.

Place a bowl under a fine-mesh sieve and drain the olive oil from the olive confit. Reserve the oil. Place the olives, lemons, shallots, and thyme sprigs in a clean bowl. Spoon ¼ cup (60 ml) of the olive confit oil over the top. Measure out roughly another 2 tablespoons of the oil and set aside. (Store the remaining oil in a glass jar in the fridge. It will have a mild lemon, garlic, and olive flavor and can be used in any recipe that calls for olive oil.)

To make the whipped ricotta and cream cheese, place all of the ingredients in a food processor and blend until well combined. Spoon into a bowl.

Lightly drizzle the remaining 1½ tablespoons or so of olive confit oil over the slices of bread. In a skillet over low heat, toast the bread for 5–10 minutes each side, until golden and crispy. Serve with the olive confit and whipped ricotta and cream cheese.

SERVES 4

OLIVE CONFIT

1 garlic head

Boiling water

2⅔ cups (350 g) pitted green olives

2¼ cups (300 g) pitted kalamata olives

1 lemon, quartered

2 cups (500 ml) extra-virgin olive oil

2 shallots, peeled and halved

5 thyme sprigs

Pinch of sea salt

WHIPPED RICOTTA & CREAM CHEESE

7 oz (200 g) cream cheese

6 tablespoons (100 g) ricotta

Grated zest of 1 lemon

1 tablespoon lemon juice

2 teaspoons oil from the olive confit, plus 2 tablespoons for drizzling

2 teaspoons honey

Pinch of sea salt

Pinch of freshly ground black pepper

FOR SERVING

4 slices No-Knead Bread (page 127)

Roasted bell peppers are surprisingly easy to prepare. I use the word "surprisingly" as this is one of those dishes that my mum would always make and, when I asked her how it was done, I was—for lack of a better word—surprised. I even questioned her method, asking, "Are you sure that's all you do?" The thing that makes these roasted bell peppers extra special is the use of high-quality extra-virgin olive oil. And lots of it. The bell peppers are delicious as is, but can also be turned into a delectable spread for sandwiches or blended with tomato confit for a soup.

ALSO USED IN:

- Tomato & garlic confit soup with grilled cheese .31
- The ultimate Italian deli sandwich 118
- Chorizo fat–fried eggs with crispy potatoes 156

Roasted bell peppers

Preheat the oven to 425°F. Line a baking sheet with parchment paper.

Place the bell peppers on the prepared sheet and bake for 1 hour, flipping the bell peppers over once or twice. Their skin should begin to char and blacken.

Place the bell peppers in a large bowl and cover with plastic wrap or a clean kitchen towel. Let sit for 30 minutes to allow the bell peppers to steam and slightly cool. Remove the bell peppers from the bowl, peel off their skins, and remove the seeds.

Place the flesh of the bell peppers in a clean bowl with the olive oil, garlic (if using), and a little salt and pepper. Top with a sprinkling of basil leaves, if desired.

SERVES 8

6 large red bell peppers

¼ cup (60 ml) extra-virgin olive oil

1 garlic clove (optional), minced

Sea salt

Freshly ground black pepper

Basil leaves (optional)

TIP

Store leftovers in an airtight container in the fridge for up to 1 week. Take out of the fridge at least 20 minutes before using to allow the olive oil to reliquefy.

On special occasions like a birthday or Christmas Eve dinner, my mum would always ask us what we wanted to eat and, without fail, my brother and I would respond with "Rosemarys." What I can tell you is that Rosemarys are bread-stuffed eggplants. What I can't tell you is why we call them Rosemarys. We have no memory as to why they were affectionately given this name; it's just one of those things. Made with the most delicious stuffing of eggplant, breadcrumbs, oregano, egg, and garlic, our family secret is to create indents in the stuffing and pour olive oil into them. The olive oil further flavors the bread stuffing and also helps to create a beautiful golden and crunchy crust. Paired with my tomato and basil sauce, this meal has been on high rotation in our family for years, and I promise it will be in yours, too.

Rosemarys (bread-stuffed eggplants)

3 eggplants

¼ cup (60 ml) extra-virgin olive oil, plus more for drizzling

Sea salt

6 slices stale white bread (about 10½ oz/300 g)

1 tablespoon dried oregano

3 garlic cloves, minced

2 eggs

Freshly ground black pepper

2 cups (480 ml) Tomato & Basil Sauce (page 55), warmed, for serving

Grated Pecorino Romano, for serving

Preheat the oven to 400°F. Line a baking sheet with parchment paper.

Halve the eggplants lengthwise. Place them on the prepared baking sheet, cut side up, and lightly drizzle with some olive oil and a sprinkling of salt. Bake for 20 minutes.

Take the eggplants out of the oven. They should be soft to touch but still have a slight spring to them. Let cool slightly. Lower the oven temperature to 350°F.

Using a spoon, scoop the flesh out of the eggplant shells: Do this by following the shape of the eggplant around the edges, then scoop out the eggplant flesh. Don't worry if a few holes or tears are made in the skin. Set 5 eggplant shells aside, then finely chop the remaining eggplant shell and set aside.

Place the slices of white bread in a blender and process until you have a fine and crumbly texture. Place in a large bowl and add the oregano, garlic, eggs, a pinch of salt and pepper, the eggplant flesh, and the chopped eggplant shell. Combine all the ingredients by mixing them together with your hands and using a squeezing motion.

Place the 5 eggplant shells on a clean baking sheet lined with fresh parchment paper. Evenly distribute the eggplant filling among the eggplant shells—fill them as tightly as you can. Using your index finger, make three indents roughly 1½ inches (4 cm) deep in the filling in each shell and drizzle the ¼ cup (60 ml) olive oil into them.

Bake the eggplant shells for 30 minutes, or until golden and crispy on top.

Serve immediately, with the warm tomato and basil sauce and a sprinkling of Pecorino Romano.

SERVES 5

There is nothing new or exciting about this pesto recipe. It's just a great-tasting, traditionally made pesto that is incomparable to the store-bought stuff from the supermarket. I make it using a mortar and pestle, but you can easily make it in a food processor on those days you aren't quite up for an arm workout. This pesto is perfectly paired with light and fluffy ricotta gnocchi, which is potato gnocchi's low-maintenance counterpart.

ALSO USED IN:
- *The ultimate Italian deli sandwich.........................118*
- *Tomato & pesto toast topper.... 129*

Pesto genovese with ricotta gnocchi

To make the pesto, submerge the basil leaves in a bowl of ice water for 5 minutes. Remove from the ice bath and pat dry with paper towels.

Place the garlic cloves and salt in a mortar and crush with the pestle until a paste-like texture forms. Add the pine nuts and pound until they are broken down but still have some texture to them. Add the basil leaves in three or four batches and pound until you have a bright green paste.

Add the Pecorino Romano and parmesan in three batches and gently mix them in. Pour in the olive oil and stir until the pesto is at a consistency you like.

To make the ricotta gnocchi, place all of the ingredients, except the flour, in a large bowl and mix with your hands or a wooden spoon to combine. Slowly incorporate the flour until a soft ball forms. You may not need to use all of the flour if your ricotta is very dry. If your dough is too wet or sticky, add a little more flour.

Lightly dust a wooden board or work surface with flour and tip the dough onto it. Very gently knead the dough into a smooth ball. Using a sharp knife, cut the dough into 6 equal portions.

Using the palms of your hands, roll each portion of dough into a sausage shape, roughly ½ inch (1.5 cm) thick. Cut the gnocchi pieces into your desired size. I like to cut them ½ inch (1.5 cm) wide. Place the gnocchi on a baking sheet or large plate that has been lightly dusted with flour and cover with a clean kitchen towel. Repeat until you have made all of the gnocchi.

Bring a large saucepan of heavily salted water to a boil. Place the gnocchi in the boiling water and cook for 2–3 minutes, until they have risen to the top. Drain the gnocchi, reserving 1 cup (240 ml) of the cooking water.

Return the gnocchi to the pan, along with the pesto. Slowly incorporate the cooking water until you have a smooth, silky, and glossy texture. Serve immediately, with a sprinkling of Pecorino Romano.

SERVES 4–6

PESTO

1 bunch of basil (about 2¼ oz/60 g), leaves picked

Ice water

2 garlic cloves, peeled but whole

Pinch of sea salt

⅓ cup (40 g) pine nuts

3 tablespoons grated Pecorino Romano, plus more for serving

3 tablespoons grated parmesan

¾ cup (180 ml) extra-virgin olive oil

RICOTTA GNOCCHI

1¾ cups (450 g) ricotta

⅓ cup (40 g) grated parmesan

2 egg yolks

Pinch of sea salt

Pinch of freshly ground black pepper

1¾ cups (200 g) tipo "00" flour, plus more for dusting

TIP

To make the pesto in a food processor, blend the garlic, salt, pine nuts, and basil leaves until well combined, but still with some texture. Stir in the cheese and olive oil and serve.

My partner comes from a very large family. When I was little, I longed to have a big family like his. I fantasized about long tables filled with food as far as your eyes could see for my imaginary large family and me to gather around. Now that I have been welcomed into a large family, that dream is clearly not the reality. Yes, it's lovely to make it happen every now and then but, actually, it's hard work cooking for a big group of people—especially when you're the cook in the family. Enter my baked pasta. I love this meal for many reasons, including the use of my rich tomato and basil sauce, crispy olive oil–baked eggplant, and ricotta spooned on top. But what I love most about this dish is that it will always happily feed a large group of people . . . or if making just for yourself or small family, you will have plenty of leftovers to enjoy throughout the week.

SERVE WITH:

Basil olive oil 51

Baked pasta with crispy eggplant & ricotta

1 eggplant

Sea salt

½ cup (120 ml) extra-virgin olive oil

1 teaspoon dried oregano

1 lb (500 g) rigatoni

1 quart (1 liter) Tomato & Basil Sauce (page 51), hot

2 tablespoons grated parmesan

1½ cups (150 g) shredded mozzarella

1 cup (250 g) ricotta

Basil leaves, for serving

Slice the eggplant crosswise into rounds roughly ¾ inch (2 cm) thick. Place into a colander and sprinkle with a very generous amount of salt on both sides. Let rest for 30–45 minutes to remove the moisture.

Preheat the oven to 400°F. Line a baking sheet with parchment paper.

Rinse the eggplant slices under cold water to remove the salt. Place onto paper towels and pat dry as much as possible.

In a shallow bowl, combine the olive oil and oregano. Dip the eggplant slices into the olive oil for 1–2 seconds on each side and place onto the prepared baking sheet.

Bake for 20 minutes or until crispy and golden, ensuring you check on them as some will cook faster than others.

While the eggplant slices are baking, cook the rigatoni in a large saucepan of heavily salted boiling water. Drain the pasta 2 minutes before the suggested cooking time as it will continue to cook when it's stirred into the sauce. Reserve ½–1 cup (120–240 ml) of the pasta cooking water.

In a Dutch oven over medium heat, combine the hot tomato and basil sauce with the pasta. Slowly incorporate the reserved pasta water until you have a smooth and glossy texture. Place the crispy eggplants on top. Sprinkle with the parmesan, followed by the mozzarella. Dollop the ricotta. Transfer to the oven.

Bake for 20–25 minutes, until the cheese has melted and is golden and bubbling.

Finish with some basil leaves and a drizzle of basil olive oil, then serve.

SERVES 6

Right before my thirty-fourth birthday, I was struck down with tonsillitis. And being the birthday girl that I am, I was feeling very sorry for myself. My partner loves to spoil me on my birthday and, while he was offering to buy me a fancy sushi platter, oysters, and even lobster rolls, all I wanted was my mum's fish soup. It will cure any aliment, from tonsillitis to a broken heart. It's one of those meals that will always feel like a big warm hug from my mum, which is exactly what the doctor ordered. I have suggested you make this soup with a firm white fish, but salmon, shrimp, or even mussels work perfectly, too.

Mum's fish soup

Cut the fish into large pieces and lightly season with salt and pepper on both sides.

Heat the olive oil in a large saucepan over low heat, then sauté the onion and garlic for 5 minutes, or until fragrant and translucent. Increase the heat to medium and add the tomatoes, a generous amount of salt and pepper, and sugar (if using). Cook for 5 minutes, or until the mixture is jammy and soft.

Deglaze the pan with the white wine and cook until 80 percent of the wine has evaporated. Add the stock and bring to a boil. Decrease the heat to low and simmer for 10–15 minutes, uncovered. Season to taste with salt and pepper.

Add the fish to the pan and cook over medium-high heat for 3–4 minutes, until the fish is firm and opaque in color. Test one piece by cutting it in half before taking the pan off the heat.

Finish the soup with a sprinkling of parsley and dill, then divide among bowls and serve.

SERVES 4

1 lb 5 oz (300 g) firm white
   fish, such as cod

Sea salt

Freshly ground black pepper

⅓ cup (80 ml) extra-virgin olive oil

1 onion, finely diced

2 garlic cloves, minced

2 tomatoes, diced

1–2 teaspoons sugar (optional)

½ cup (120 ml) white wine

2 cups (480 ml) chicken
   or fish stock

Handful of flat-leaf parsley
   leaves, finely chopped

Handful of dill fronds,
   finely chopped

TIP
Use very ripe tomatoes for this soup, so they are juicy and sweet.

Pairing an already rich and oily piece of fish with tomatoes that have been slow-cooked in lots of fat works very well. This recipe was created when my friend Steph was unexpectedly visiting for lunch and I needed to quickly throw something together. I had salmon, fresh herbs, and a jar of tomato confit in my fridge, as I always do. We both fell in love with this meal. So much so that it made the cut for this cookbook. Finish this off with a drizzle of tomato confit olive oil and sticky balsamic and, voilà, you've got yourself a quick yet delicious meal.

Pan-fried salmon with cherry tomato confit

2 skinless salmon fillets

Sea salt

Freshly ground black pepper

1 tablespoon extra-virgin olive oil

⅓ cup (80 g) Cherry Tomato Confit (page 52)

1 tablespoon balsamic glaze

¼ red onion, finely sliced

12 basil leaves

1½ oz (40 g) Greek feta, crumbled

Season the salmon with salt and pepper on each side. Heat the olive oil in a skillet over medium heat. Fry the salmon for 3 minutes on each side until medium-rare.

Remove the salmon from the pan and transfer to a serving plate. Drain off as much oil as possible from the cherry tomato confit and spoon over the salmon. Follow this with a drizzle of the reserved oil and the balsamic glaze. Sprinkle the red onion, basil leaves, and feta on top and serve immediately.

SERVES 2

Pasta puttanesca was the first dish I learned to make on my own. While I loved to eat the food my mum made, cooking wasn't something I got into until later in life. Since I adore anchovies, olives, and tomatoes, I took up the task of teaching myself how to make puttanesca. While it's still one of my favorite meals to eat, I enjoy experimenting with these flavor combinations to come up with recipes like this one-pan roasted fish puttanesca. The tomatoes are slow-cooked to give them that jammy texture and sweet taste, with the added bonus of the anchovies, olives, and capers that melt into the sauce. Make sure you have some fresh focaccia on hand to mop up every last drop.

One-pan roasted fish puttanesca

Preheat the oven to 325°F.

In a large baking dish, combine the tomatoes, olives, anchovies, capers, and red onion. Drizzle with the olive oil and balsamic glaze and season well with salt and pepper. Toss to combine. Transfer to the oven.

Bake for 30 minutes, or until the tomatoes have burst open and are jammy.

Increase the oven temperature to 400°F.

Pat the fish dry and season well with salt and pepper on both sides.

Push aside the tomatoes in the baking dish to make room for the fish. Place the fish fillets in the empty space in the dish. Bake for 8–10 minutes, depending on the thickness of your fish, until it's cooked through. It will no longer be glassy and translucent and you should be able to push a fork through it with ease.

Sprinkle with chives and serve immediately, with a drizzle of Italian-style chile oil and some focaccia, if desired.

SERVES 4

14 oz (400 g) cherry tomatoes

1 cup (150 g) pitted kalamata olives

6 anchovy fillets

2 tablespoons capers, drained

1 red onion, finely sliced

¼ cup (60 ml) extra-virgin olive oil

1 tablespoon balsamic glaze

Sea salt

Freshly ground black pepper

4 small or 2 large fillets firm white fish, such as cod or snapper (1 lb 5 oz/600 g total)

Snipped chives or finely chopped flat-leaf parsley, for serving

A few people have admitted to me that they were a little cautious about making this recipe when they saw how much olive oil was used. Yes, it is a lot of olive oil, which should come as no surprise to you by now. However, every last drop is needed! We are not in the olive oil–wasting business here. Cooking salmon at a low temperature for a long amount of time in lots of olive oil creates the most melt-in-your-mouth texture and the salmon will fall apart at the slightest touch. This meal is simple, impressive, and luxurious. If you have leftovers, use them up in a salad or on a bagel.

ALSO USED IN:

• *Citrus salmon bagel* *125*

Salmon confit with citrus & herbs

2½ lb (1.2 kg) side of skinless salmon

Sea salt

Freshly ground black pepper

¼ teaspoon chile flakes

1 cup (240 ml) extra-virgin olive oil

1 lemon

1 lime, thinly sliced

½ orange, thinly sliced

2 tablespoons plus honey

7 oz (200 g) arugula

1½ cups (30 g) dill fronds

Preheat the oven to 275°F.

Place the salmon on an unlined sheet pan. Season the salmon with salt, pepper, and the chile flakes and massage them into the flesh. Pour the olive oil over the fish.

Thinly slice about half the lemon and save the other half for squeezing. Place the lemon, lime, and orange slices on top of the salmon. Drizzle the honey all over and transfer to the oven.

Bake for 15–20 minutes, until the salmon has turned pink on the outside.

Combine the arugula and dill in a bowl and dress with a little olive oil from the baking sheet, a squeeze of lemon, and a pinch of salt and pepper. Toss well.

Carefully remove the salmon from the baking sheet and transfer to a serving platter. Scatter the arugula and dill around the salmon and serve immediately. It is also delicious served cold the next day.

SERVES 8

TIP
Reserve the remaining olive oil and use it when cooking fish. It will have a slight salmon flavor.

There's not much to say about this dish other than it's incredibly easy to make, results in the crispiest chicken skin, and creates a sauce that is so good you might want to drink it. This is a great midweek meal for those nights when you don't feel like cooking.

One-pan crispy chicken thighs with caramelized onions & lemon

Place the chicken thighs in a large bowl with the olive oil, spices, herbs, and a generous amount of salt and pepper. Massage the mixture into the chicken. Cover the bowl and let marinate in the fridge for a minimum of 2 hours, but ideally overnight.

Bring the chicken to room temperature.

Preheat the oven to 400°F.

Place the chicken in a cold, shallow enameled cast-iron Dutch oven or braiser, skin side down. Set over medium heat and cook for 13 minutes. Place the lemon and onion under the chicken and cook for 4 minutes more.

Slightly tilt the pan and spoon out some of the chicken fat. (I use this chicken fat in my chicken broth or to fry eggs.)

Flip the chicken over so it's skin side up, then bake in the oven for 15 minutes.

Sprinkle with parsley and serve immediately.

SERVES 4

6 bone-in, skin-on chicken thighs (2¼–2½ lb/1–1.2 kg total)

2 tablespoons extra-virgin olive oil

1 tablespoon onion powder

1 tablespoon garlic powder

1 teaspoon fennel seeds

2 teaspoons dried thyme

2 teaspoons dried oregano

½ teaspoon dried parsley

Sea salt

Freshly ground black pepper

2 lemon slices

2 onions, sliced into rounds

Handful of flat-leaf parsley leaves, finely chopped

TIP

Use the leftover olive brine from my Olive Confit (page 62) to brine the chicken the day before you season it. This will create the juiciest chicken! In a large bowl, combine the chicken, olive brine, 2 peeled garlic cloves, and 4 thyme sprigs. Cover and let marinate in the fridge overnight. When ready to cook, remove the chicken from the brine and pat dry with paper towels.

While this looks and sounds like a salsa verde, I feel more comfortable calling it a green herb sauce, as it lacks a few traditional ingredients. When it really comes down to it, you can make this sauce however you please. Use whatever herbs you have in your fridge, leave out or double the anchovies, opt for shallots instead of garlic. The choice is yours, but no matter what, you will always be left with a salty, zesty, and fresh sauce that will bring any dish to life. Lamb and salsa verde are a match made in heaven, as the fresh herb sauce beautifully balances a fatty lamb chop. And if you're looking at this recipe thinking, "Why didn't she have the butcher French the chops?" it's because I love nothing more than chewing on a fatty lamb bone. It's extremely satisfying.

Lamb chops with green herb sauce

10–12 lamb rib chops
    (not Frenched), at room
    temperature
Sea salt
Freshly ground black pepper
Extra-virgin olive oil

GREEN HERB SAUCE

1 garlic clove, peeled but whole
Sea salt
2 anchovy fillets
1½ tablespoons capers, drained
1 bunch of flat-leaf parsley (about
    1½ oz/40 g), leaves picked
    and very finely chopped
1 tablespoon lemon juice
½ cup (120 ml) extra-virgin olive oil

Season the lamb chops with salt and pepper on both sides. Pat the seasoning into the meat, then lightly drizzle each side with olive oil.

To prepare the green herb sauce, place the garlic clove and a big pinch of salt in a mortar. Use the pestle to grind the garlic and salt until a paste-like texture forms. Add the anchovies and grind them into the garlic paste. Add the capers and pound until they are slightly broken down. Add the parsley and mix it in.

Pour the lemon juice and olive oil into the mortar and gently mix until all the ingredients are well combined. Taste the sauce and adjust the seasoning to your liking, if needed.

Drizzle 2 teaspoons of olive oil into a large skillet over high heat. Place the lamb chops in the pan and cook for 3 minutes on each side or until golden brown. Do not overcrowd the pan—cook in batches, if needed. Each chop may be a different thickness and size so it's best to test them all to see if they're cooked. If they feel like the fleshy bottom part of your thumb, they will be medium-rare, which is just right. Let rest for 5 minutes.

Place the lamb chops on a platter and drizzle the green herb sauce over them, then serve.

SERVES 4

Whenever my mum makes this soup, she pours it into a big mug and drinks it while curled up on the couch, repeating the same line back to me: "This soup is as popular as a milkshake."

SERVE WITH:

● *Focaccia* *112*

Mum's butternut squash soup

In a food processor, blend the butternut squash until very fine. Set aside.

In a large pot, heat ¼ cup (60 ml) of the olive oil over medium heat. Add the garlic and onion and cook for 5 minutes or until fragrant and translucent. Stir often to ensure the garlic and onion do not burn.

Add the butternut squash to the pot and the remaining ¼ cup (60 ml) olive oil. Cook for 12–15 minutes, until the butternut squash is caramelized and soft, stirring often so it doesn't stick. If there is some browning, scrape it up with a wooden spoon.

Add the bouillon cube, milk, and rosemary sprig to the pot. Once simmering, decrease the heat to low. Season with a generous amount of salt and pepper. Simmer for 15 minutes with the lid on or until the soup has slightly reduced.

Remove the rosemary sprig from the soup. Using an immersion blender, blend the soup until very smooth. Taste to ensure it is seasoned to your liking.

Ladle the soup into bowls and serve with a drizzle of olive oil and slices of focaccia.

SERVES 6

1 lb 14 oz (850 g) butternut squash, peeled and cut into 1¼-inch (3 cm) cubes

½ cup (120 ml) extra-virgin olive oil, plus more for drizzling

4 garlic cloves, finely diced

1 yellow onion, finely diced

1 chicken bouillon cube

3 cups (720 ml) whole milk

1 rosemary sprig

Sea salt

Freshly ground black pepper

When tomato confit is blended together with sweet cloves of garlic confit, and a pinch of salt and pepper, the most luxuriously rich pasta sauces is created. This dish may only use a few ingredients, but this is one of those cases where less is more. It's another great recipe to have up your sleeve when you have a jar of tomato confit tucked away in the fridge.

Tomato confit pasta

Sea salt

11 oz (300 g) penne pasta

1⅔ cups (400 g) Cherry Tomato Confit (page 52)

6 Garlic Confit cloves (page 16)

2 tablespoons Garlic Confit oil (page 16) or Cherry Tomato Confit oil (page 52)

Freshly ground black pepper

½ cup (50 g) grated Pecorino Romano

Fresh basil

2 teaspoons Italian-Style Chile Oil (optional) (page 50)

Bring a large pot of heavily salted water to a boil. Add the pasta and cook to 2–3 minutes shy of the time in the package directions. Reserving 1 cup (240 ml) of pasta water, drain the pasta.

While the pasta cooks, combine the cherry tomato confit, garlic confit cloves, and confit oil in a blender and blend until very smooth. Transfer to a skillet and season with salt and pepper. Bring to a gentle simmer over medium-low heat and cook for 5 minutes, or until the sauce is heated through and the flavors are well combined.

Add the pasta to the pan. Slowly incorporate the pasta water and the Pecorino Romano until you have a silky and glossy texture. You may not need all of the pasta water, so add it slowly.

Serve immediately with a sprinkling of fresh basil and chile oil, if desired.

SERVES 4

Without sounding too arrogant, I make the best roast chicken you will ever eat. My chicken always has the juiciest meat and a beautiful golden-brown skin. And surprisingly, you don't need a lot of ingredients to achieve this. While I adore my garlic butter whole roasted chicken with jammy shallots, sometimes I look for a chicken recipe that is a little less lavish and a little more on the simple side. Sometimes simplicity is key! I also love to roast chicken with leeks, making sure I use all parts of the plant. The top becomes crispy, almost like chips, and the bottom white part is soft and jammy.

SERVE WITH

🌿 *Green herb sauce from lamb chops with green herb sauce* 83

◉ *Focaccia* 112

Olive oil–roasted chicken

Pat the chicken skin dry with paper towels and generously season with salt and pepper all over, not forgetting the cavity. If time allows, place the chicken in the fridge and let rest, uncovered, overnight. This step acts like a dry brine and results in juicy chicken.

Remove the chicken from the fridge 30 to 60 minutes prior to cooking.

Preheat the oven to 350°F.

Using your fingers, carefully separate the skin from the chicken breast and evenly stuff with the butter. Season the chicken with the fennel seeds and more salt and pepper. Drizzle the olive oil all over the chicken and massage well with your hands.

Using a sharp knife, slice the top off the garlic bulb, about 1 inch (2.5 cm) down from the top, to expose the raw cloves, then place in the cavity of the chicken with the lemon and fresh herbs. Tie the legs of the chicken together with kitchen twine as this will help the chicken cook evenly.

Transfer the chicken a wire rack that can fit in a sheet pan. Place the leeks on the sheet pan and season with a pinch of salt and pepper. Place the wire rack that is holding the chicken over the leeks and transfer to the oven.

Bake for 1 hour 20 minutes, or until the chicken is cooked through and golden brown.

Allow the chicken to rest for 10 minutes before carving. Serve with green herb sauce (page 83) and focaccia.

SERVES 6

1 whole chicken (3 lb 5 oz/1.5 kg)

Sea salt

Freshly ground black pepper

1½ tablespoons salted butter at room temperature

1 teaspoon fennel seeds

¼ cup (60 ml) extra-virgin olive oil

1 garlic head

½ lemon

½ cup mixed fresh herbs, such as parsley, thyme, sage, rosemary

1 leek, quartered lengthwise

TIP
Brine the chicken the day before using the leftover buttermilk from making my Homemade Butter (page 92).

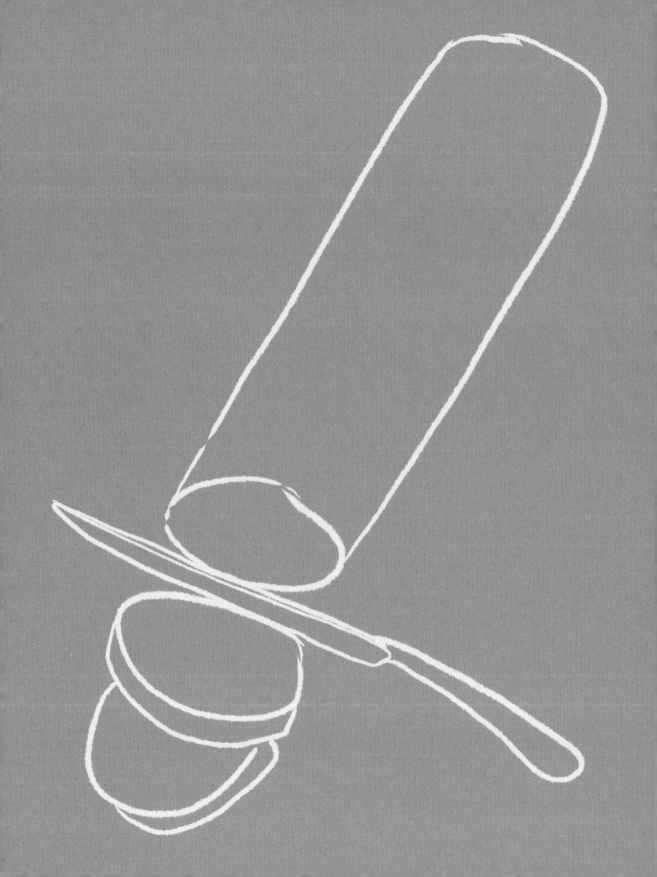

3

Butter

Homemade butter
Mushroom pie with garlic confit & sour cream puff pastry
Fennel & lemon risotto
Caramelized onion & goat cheese galette
Pasta alla vodka
White wine butter mussels with triple cooked french fries
Whole roasted snapper with green anchovy butter
Pastina with homemade chicken broth
Garlic butter cheesy muffins

Making your own butter is one of those things that is surprisingly easy to do. All you need is cream and a stand mixer. You could churn butter by hand, but it takes a lot of patience and whipping—hats off to you if you decide to go down that path! Spread your fresh butter onto a piece of a freshly baked bread that is still warm from the oven and enter buttery carb heaven.

SERVE WITH:

○ *No-knead bread* *127*

Homemade butter

Pour the heavy cream into the bowl of a stand mixer fitted with a paddle attachment. On low speed, whip the cream until it begins to thicken. Increase the speed to medium-high and whip for 5–7 minutes. At first the cream will turn into whipped cream, then the buttermilk (liquid) will begin to break away from the butter (fat/solids).

Remove the butter from the mixer and reserve the buttermilk for another use (see Tip). Rinse the butter in ice water and squeeze out as much of the buttermilk as possible.

If you would like salted butter, sprinkle a work surface with flaky sea salt and roll the butter over it.

Place the butter on a large piece of parchment paper and roll into a tight log. Store in the fridge and use within 2 weeks.

2 cups (480 ml) heavy cream
Ice water
Flaky sea salt

MAKES 8½ OZ (240 G)

TIP

Don't throw away the buttermilk! Store it in a sterilized jar in the fridge and use within a few days to brine my Olive Oil–Roasted Chicken (page 88) with.

This pie is the meal I envision myself making in a quaint country home with timber-framed windows that open onto rolling mountains. The pie is so rustic with its uneven edges—that I can picture it perfectly.

Mushroom pie with garlic confit & sour cream puff pastry

3 tablespoons extra-virgin olive oil

7 tablespoons (100 g) unsalted butter

7 oz (200 g) brown mushrooms, sliced

7 oz (200 g) shiitake mushrooms, sliced

2 shallots, finely diced

4 garlic cloves, minced

½ cup (120 ml) white wine

4 thyme sprigs

1 cup (240 ml) chicken or vegetable stock

Sea salt

Freshly ground black pepper

⅔ cup (160 ml) heavy cream

½ bunch of flat-leaf parsley, finely chopped

Juice of ½ lemon

All-purpose flour, for dusting

Garlic Confit & Sour Cream Puff Pastry (page 23)

Egg wash: 1 egg, whisked

Heat 1½ tablespoons of the olive oil and half the butter in a large heavy-bottomed skillet over medium heat. Once the butter has melted and there is a slight sizzle from the pan, add the mushrooms and cook, undisturbed, for 3 minutes. Stir the mushrooms and cook for 5 minutes more, or until browned and slightly caramelized. Remove the mushrooms from the pan and set aside on a plate.

Decrease the heat to medium-low and add the remaining 1½ tablespoons olive oil and remaining butter to the pan. Cook the shallots and garlic for 5–7 minutes, stirring regularly to prevent the garlic from burning. Deglaze the pan with the white wine and cook for 2 minutes or until 80 percent of the liquid has evaporated.

Return the mushrooms to the pan, along with the thyme and stock, and season generously with salt and pepper. Increase the heat to medium-high and cook at a rapid boil for 5 minutes, or until the liquid has reduced by two-thirds. Decrease the heat to low and add the heavy cream. Cook for several minutes, stirring occasionally, until you have a thick consistency.

Remove the pan from the heat. Discard the thyme stems. Stir in the parsley and lemon juice. Transfer the mixture to a bowl and let cool in the fridge for 20 minutes.

Preheat the oven to 350°F.

On a lightly flour dusted work surface, roll out half of the pastry into a large round that is ¹⁄₁₆ inch (2 mm) thick and 10 inches (25 cm) wide. Transfer to a baking sheet lined with parchment paper. Roll out the remaining pastry into a slightly larger round—about 12 inches (30 cm) wide.

Spoon the cooled mushroom filling over the puff pastry on the baking sheet, leaving a ¾-inch (2 cm) border around the edge. Place the second sheet of puff pastry over the top and crimp the edges together with a fork. Brush the pastry all over with the egg wash. Using a sharp knife, make 4 incisions 2 inches (5 cm) long in the center on top of the pie.

Bake for 20–25 minutes, until golden and crispy. Let rest for 15 minutes before slicing and serving.

SERVES 6

In my high school years, there was a joke among my friends and me that if a day of the week were to best describe me, it would be Sunday. I love a slow day where I spend a good part of it in my pajamas and on the couch while eating something extremely comforting. Risotto is my Sunday meal. It's pure comfort food that will always make me feel nourished and happy. When making a risotto, I like to keep the flavors as simple and delicate as possible. This is quite a traditional risotto, but with a little contemporary twist from the lemon that brings a lovely fresh zestiness to a rich base of white wine, butter, and Pecorino Romano.

Fennel & lemon risotto

Finely slice the fennel using a mandoline or a very sharp knife. Reserve the leaves from the fennel fronds.

Heat the olive oil in a large saucepan over low heat. Fry the shallots, sliced fennel, and garlic for 10 minutes, or until translucent and fragrant, stirring occasionally.

Increase the heat to medium, add the rice to the pan, and cook for 2 minutes, or until the rice becomes opaque. Add the wine and keep stirring until it has been absorbed by the rice.

Add 1 cup (240 ml) of the chicken stock and stir until all the stock has been absorbed. Repeat this step five more times, until you have used up all the stock. The rice will start to become plump as it continues to cook and absorb the stock. It should take roughly 25 minutes to cook. When you have added the last 1 cup (240 ml) of stock, you want about 80 percent of the liquid to have been absorbed.

Decrease the heat to low, add the butter, pecorino, lemon zest, lemon juice, and a generous amount of salt and pepper and stir them in.

Take the risotto off the heat and sprinkle the reserved fennel fronds over the top. Serve immediately.

SERVES 4

1 large fennel bulb

¼ cup (60 ml) extra-virgin olive oil

2 shallots, finely diced

4 garlic cloves, minced

1 cup plus 2 tablespoons (220 g) Arborio rice

½ cup (120 ml) white wine

6⅓ cups (1.5 liters) chicken stock

3½ tablespoons (50 g) unsalted butter

6 tablespoons (45 g) grated Pecorino Romano

Grated zest of 1 lemon

1 tablespoon plus lemon juice

Sea salt

Freshly ground black pepper

When it comes to cooking caramelized onions, you need to know two things: Cook low and cook slow. Unfortunately, there is no way around this and, contrary to what some people may think, they aren't caramelized onions unless they have been cooking in the pan for at least 45 minutes (a little less if you need them for a soup or stew). I like to pop them in the pan, then I'll hop in the bath and get my partner, Joel, to stir the onions every 10 minutes or so. This is the extent of Joel's cooking skills. (You will usually hear me yelling from the bathroom, "Have you stirred the onions?") I also like to drizzle balsamic glaze onto my onions during the final part of cooking to get them nice and sweet and sticky. They pair perfectly with goat cheese and, as this is such a rich meal, I like to top my galette with some lemon juice and arugula.

Caramelized onion & goat cheese galette

CARAMELIZED ONIONS

2 teaspoons extra-virgin olive oil

4 tablespoons (50 g) unsalted butter

4 onions, finely sliced

Sea salt

2 teaspoons balsamic glaze

GALETTE

All-purpose flour, for dusting

½ recipe Garlic Confit & Sour Cream Puff Pastry (page 23)

2¼ oz (60 g) goat cheese

4 thyme sprigs, leaves picked

Egg wash: 1 egg, whisked

Juice of ½ lemon

Large handful of arugula (optional)

To make the caramelized onions, heat the olive oil and butter in a deep, heavy-bottomed saucepan over medium heat. When sizzling, add the onions. Immediately decrease the heat to low and cook for 45 minutes, stirring occasionally.

Once the onion is golden brown, season with a generous amount of salt and drizzle with the balsamic glaze. Cook for 15 minutes more, stirring occasionally. Take off the heat and set aside.

Preheat the oven to 350°F. Line a baking sheet with parchment paper.

Sprinkle your work surface with flour. Using a rolling pin, roll the pastry out to a large round that is roughly ⅛ inch (4 mm) thick and 10 inches (25 cm) wide. Roll the pastry onto the rolling pin, then lay it over the prepared baking sheet.

Evenly spread the caramelized onions over the puff pastry, leaving a 1½-inch (4 cm) border. Break apart the goat cheese and crumble it over the onions. Sprinkle the thyme leaves over the cheese.

Fold the pastry border over the filling, pinching the pastry together to form a rustic circle shape. Brush the egg wash over all of the pastry. This will help give the pastry a lovely golden color. Bake for 15–20 minutes, until golden and crispy.

Let the galette rest for 15 minutes. Squeeze the lemon juice over the top, scatter the arugula (if using), and serve.

SERVES 4

While it would be hard to go wrong with this combination of ingredients, the secret to a successful vodka sauce is to fry off the tomato paste until it turns a deep-red color, is sticking to the pan, and has caramelized. The vodka sweetens the tomato paste and enhances the fruity flavor within the sauce. But the magic really happens when the sauce is brought together by stirring in the butter and cheese it with lots of pasta water, as you will create the silkiest, glossiest, and creamiest of sauces. Pasta water is liquid gold and should always be utilized when making any pasta sauce.

SERVE WITH:

🌿 *Italian-style chile oil 50*

Pasta alla vodka

If using dried pasta, cook this first. Bring a saucepan of heavily salted water to a boil and cook the pasta for 2–3 minutes less than the instructions on the package, as it will continue to cook when it's stirred into the sauce. Reserve ¾ –1 cup (120–240 ml) of the pasta cooking water.

Heat the olive oil in an enameled cast-iron Dutch oven over low heat and fry the onion and garlic for 5 minutes or until fragrant and translucent. Stir occasionally to prevent the garlic from burning. Add the oregano and chile flakes and fry for 2 minutes.

Turn the heat to high, add the tomato paste, and fry for 2–3 minutes, until it has caramelized, become a deep-red color, and is almost sticking to the dish. Decrease the heat to medium and add the vodka. Cook until 80 percent of the liquid has evaporated. Add the cream and cook for 1 minute or until the cream has foamed and is bubbling. Decrease the heat to low and stir the cream into the sauce with the flaky salt until all the ingredients are well combined.

If using fresh pasta, cook it now for 2 minutes in a saucepan of heavily salted boiling water. Reserve ½–1 cup (120–240 ml) of the pasta cooking water.

Add the cooked pasta to the sauce. In thirds, add the Pecorino Romano, butter, and a splash of pasta water, stirring to combine. Slowly incorporate enough pasta water until you have a silky and glossy texture. Finish with an extra sprinkling of cheese and chile flakes and serve immediately.

SERVES 4–6

Sea salt

1 lb (500 g) dried penne or
1 recipe fresh farfalle (page 164)

¼ cup (60 ml) extra-virgin olive oil

1 onion, finely diced

2 garlic cloves, minced

1 teaspoon dried oregano

½ teaspoon chile flakes,
plus more for serving

⅔ cup (140 g) tomato paste

7 tablespoons (100 ml) vodka

1 cup (240 ml) heavy cream

Pinch of flaky sea salt

6 tablespoons (45 g) grated
Pecorino Romano, plus
more for serving

4 tablespoons (50 g)
unsalted butter

For me, cooking with mussels is not only about their sweet and salty taste but also about their sound. I love listening to their shells clattering on the sides of my metal sink as I rinse them clean, or my pan rattling from side to side as the mussels cook—their shells popping open and releasing their salty brine into the sauce. This recipe is my take on a very traditional Belgian recipe, moules-frites, which translates to "mussels and fries."

White wine butter mussels with triple cooked french fries

Square off the potatoes by trimming off the edges until you have square edges. Cut the potatoes into french fry shapes that are roughly ½ × 2½ inches (2 × 6 cm).

Place the cut fries into a bowl of ice water and rinse well until the water turns cloudy. This is the starch that has been removed from the potato. Drain in a colander and rinse again under cold water.

Place the fries into a large pot and cover with cold water. Season with a generous amount of salt. Place the pot over high heat and start the timer for 20 minutes as soon as you turn the heat on. Once the water is boiling, turn the heat to medium. Cook the potatoes until they are fork-tender. Drain and place the fries on a wire rack to allow all the moisture to drip off. Place the rack into the fridge or freezer until the fries are cold, not frozen, 30 minutes in the freezer and up to 2 hours in the fridge.

To make the fries, pour the oil in a large pot and bring to 284°F (140°C). Using a slotted spoon, carefully place the fries into the hot oil and fry for 8 minutes. Using a slotted spoon, remove the fries from the oil and place back onto the wire rack. Place the fries back into the fridge or freezer until cold.

For the second fry, use the same oil but heat it to 356°F (180°C) this time. Using a slotted spoon, carefully place the fries into the hot oil and fry for 4–6 minutes or until golden and crispy. Using a slotted spoon, remove the fries from the oil and place back onto the rack. Season generously with sea salt and serve.

Debeard the mussels by pulling their beards in an upward motion away from your body until you can pull them out of the shells. Clean the shells under running water and scrub the mussels with a wire scrubber until all the barnacles have been removed.

Heat the extra-virgin olive oil in an enameled cast-iron Dutch oven and fry the shallots and garlic for 5 minutes, or until fragrant and translucent. Stir occasionally to prevent the garlic from burning.

Increase the heat to medium and add the white wine. Cook until the white wine has reduced by half.

TRIPLE COOKED FRENCH FRIES

1¾ lb (800 g) russet, Yukon Gold, or red-skinned potatoes, peeled

Ice water

2 quarts (2 liters) light extra-virgin olive oil (or a mix of light olive oil and vegetable oil)

Sea salt

MUSSELS

2¼–4½ lb (1–2 kg) mussels

1 tablespoon extra-virgin olive oil

2 shallots, finely diced

4 garlic cloves, minced

½ cup (120 ml) white wine

7 tablespoons (100 g) unsalted butter

Handful of flat-leaf parsley leaves, finely chopped

½ lemon

TIP

If you can't be bothered making the fries, simply fry some bread in olive oil or slice up some Focaccia (page 112) to scoop up all of the delicious sauce.

Decrease the heat to low and add the butter to the pot. Stir the butter into the sauce until it has completely melted.

Increase the heat to medium, add the mussels to the pot, and stir them into the sauce. Pop the lid onto the Dutch oven and let the mussels steam for 10 minutes or until all the shells have opened.

Take the mussels off the heat, sprinkle with the parsley, and squeeze the lemon juice over the top. Serve immediately with the french fries.

SERVES 4–6

I love cooking a whole fish. Sadly, whole fish have a reputation for being difficult to cook, but this could not be further from the truth. If you get your fishmonger to scale and gut the fish for you, all you have to do is season it, bake it for a short amount of time, and slather something delicious on top. I promise you, whoever you serve this to will be so impressed that they will endlessly compliment your cooking skills, even though it takes little-to-no skill to cook (but that can be our little secret).

SERVE WITH:

- *Grilled peach, tomato & burrata salad with basil olive oil* 61
- *Focaccia* 112

Whole roasted snapper with green anchovy butter

2 (14 oz/400 g) whole snapper (or 1 large one), scaled and gutted (ask your fishmonger to do this for you)

Sea salt

Freshly ground black pepper

1 lemon, thinly sliced

3 tablespoons extra-virgin olive oil

7 tablespoons Green Anchovy Butter (recipe follows)

Finely chopped flat-leaf parsley leaves, for serving

Preheat the oven to 425°F. Line a baking sheet with parchment paper.

Pat the snapper dry with paper towels. Using a sharp knife, make 3 diagonal incisions 2 inches (5 cm) long on each side of the fish—not down to the bone but enough to visibly score the flesh. Season the fish inside and out with a generous amount of salt and pepper. Stuff the cavity of the fish with the lemon slices.

Place the snapper on the lined baking sheet. Drizzle each fish with 1½ tablespoons of olive oil. Bake for 10–15 minutes, until the flesh is white and no longer translucent.

While the fish is cooking, melt the green anchovy butter in a small saucepan over low heat. Drizzle the butter over the fish, sprinkle with parsley, and serve immediately.

SERVES 4

Green anchovy butter

8 anchovy fillets

14 tablespoons (7 oz/200 g) unsalted butter, at room temperature, roughly chopped

1½ tablespoons capers, drained

1 long green chile pepper, chopped

3 cups (60 g) flat-leaf parsley leaves

2 garlic cloves, peeled but whole

1 tablespoon extra-virgin olive oil

Sea salt

Freshly ground black pepper

Place all of the ingredients in a food processor and blend until well combined. Spoon the butter onto a piece of parchment paper and roll into a tight log. Store in the fridge for several weeks.

MAKES 10 SERVINGS

TIP

The green anchovy butter is great to have in the fridge to serve with steak, lamb, fish, or even just to spread on toast.

This recipe is the most comforting meal you can eat. Whenever I am curled up on the couch with a big bowl of pastina in brodo, my heart and soul are warmed. Every spoonful of this nutritious soup transports me back to my childhood home. My mum would always make a bowl of pastina when feeling down or sick, as it is believed to banish the blues and cure a cold. I now make this meal for my two-year-old daughter at least once a week, so I like to add an egg for that extra nutritional value—however, you can leave it out, if you wish.

TIP

Use the chicken carcass from the Garlic Butter–Roasted Chicken with Jammy Shallots (page 35) to create an even richer bone broth.

Pastina with homemade chicken broth

In a saucepan over high heat, bring the chicken broth to a boil. Add the pastina and butter to the broth and immediately turn the heat down to medium-low. Continuously stir the pastina for roughly 7 minutes, or until it's plump and soft. Stir in the cheese, then take the pan off the heat.

In a small bowl, whisk the egg (if using). Add ½ cup (120 ml) of the pastina 1 tablespoon at a time to the egg, whisking each time. This will temper the egg and prevent it from scrambling. Slowly drizzle the mixture back into the pan, whisking constantly.

Season to taste with salt and pepper. Finish with a sprinkling of extra cheese and a drizzle of olive oil and serve.

SERVES 2

4 cups (1 liter) Chicken Broth (recipe follows)

1 cup (180 g) pastina

4 tablespoons (50 g) unsalted butter

¼ cup (25 g) grated Pecorino Romano or parmesan, plus more for serving

1 egg (optional)

Sea salt

Freshly ground black pepper

Extra-virgin olive oil, for serving

Chicken broth

To make the chicken broth, place all of the ingredients in a very large saucepan or a stockpot. Leave the pot uncovered and bring to a boil. Turn the heat to low so the broth is at a gentle simmer. Simmer for 1 hour.

Remove the chicken and pick off the meat with a fork. Allow the meat to cool slightly, then store in an airtight container for another use. Return the chicken carcass to the broth and partially cover the pot with a lid. Simmer gently over low heat for a minimum of 2 hours and a maximum of 6 hours.

Allow the broth to cool slightly, then strain through a fine-mesh sieve. Discard the solids. Reserve 1 quart (1 liter) of broth to cook the pastina and store the remainder in sterilized jars or an airtight container in the fridge for up to 1 week or 3 months in the freezer.

MAKES ABOUT 4 TO 6 QUARTS/LITERS

1 whole chicken (3 lb 5 oz–4½ lb/1.5–2 kg)

3 carrots, roughly chopped

3 celery stalks, roughly chopped

2 onions, unpeeled, quartered

2 teaspoons black peppercorns

1 garlic head, halved horizontally

Handful of flat-leaf parsley stalks

Handful of fennel fronds

1 tablespoon sea salt

2 dried bay leaves

5 dried shiitake mushrooms (optional)

8½ quarts (8 liters) cold water

I am a savory muffin girl! I will always choose a savory muffin over a sweet one. However, here in Australia, I am rarely given the choice. While bakeries and grocers are filled with blueberry, chocolate, or peach muffins, savory muffins are hard to come by. Us savory muffin girls are living in a sweet muffin world. This is why I chose to create my own savory muffin recipe so I'm never without them when I have those cravings. What makes this recipe extra special is the use of my garlic confit butter that seeps into every crevice of the muffin. It makes every bite taste like garlicky heaven!

Garlic butter cheesy muffins

3½ oz (75 g) Roasted Garlic Herb Butter (page 20)

1½ cups (190 g) all-purpose flour

1½ teaspoons baking powder

1½ teaspoons baking soda

Sea salt

Freshly ground black pepper

1 cup (240 ml) whole milk

1 egg

¼ cup (60 ml) extra-virgin olive oil

¼ cup (65 g) plain yogurt

1⅓ cups (150 g) grated cheddar cheese

½ cup (50 g) grated parmesan

2 scallions, finely chopped (about ¼ cup)

Preheat the oven to 350°F.

In a small pot, melt the roasted garlic herb butter over low heat. (Alternatively, place into a microwave-safe bowl and melt in 30-second bursts, stirring after each.)

Brush 9 cups of a muffin tin with half the melted roasted garlic herb butter, reserving the remaining half for when the muffins have baked.

In a large bowl, whisk together the flour, baking powder, baking soda, and a pinch of salt and pepper.

In another large bowl, whisk together the milk, egg, olive oil, and yogurt.

Combine the wet and dry ingredients, mixing with a spatula until just combined. Gently fold in the grated cheddar, parmesan, and scallions. The batter will be thick and sticky.

Divide the batter among the 9 muffin cups, roughly 2 tablespoons of mixture per cup.

Bake for 20–22 minutes, until the muffins are golden and crispy on the edges and a skewer comes out dry when poked into the middle. Remove the muffins from the tin and place onto a wire rack.

Brush the remaining roasted garlic herb butter all over the muffins while they are still hot. Let cool for 5 minutes before eating.

MAKES 9 MUFFINS

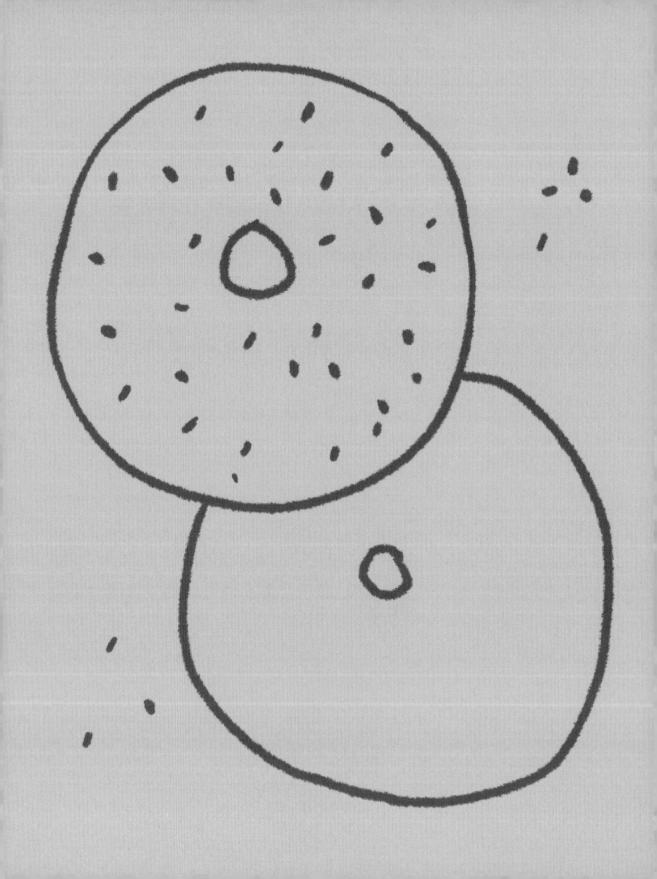

4

Bread

A good focaccia needs lots of good-quality olive oil. There is olive oil in the dough, in the bowl it rises in, in the baking pan it bakes in, and it is drizzled on top of the bread before baking. There is even olive oil rubbed all over your fingers to dimple the dough. If you're here, you're clearly an olive oil lover yourself, and if there was one recipe I could dedicate to all the olive oil fans out there, it would be this one. While I have become known for my no-knead focaccia recipe (look that one up on my website), this is more of a traditional focaccia that requires a stand mixer and lots of kneading—20 minutes to be exact. But I promise it's worth the wait and that little bit of extra effort. The center is light and fluffy and the exterior is golden and crispy thanks to all of that olive oil we use.

ALSO USED IN:
- Three focaccia sandwiches 118

Focaccia

Combine the yeast, water, and honey in a bowl and mix until well combined. Let rest for 5 minutes. The yeast will feed off the honey and become active. Once you see bubbles and foam starting to form on the top, the yeast is active and ready to use.

In a stand mixer fitted with a dough hook, combine the flour and salt. Mix on low speed for 30 seconds. Turn the mixer off and add the yeast mixture. Mix on low speed for 10 minutes or until a sticky dough forms. You may need to scrape down the sides of the bowl to ensure all the flour is incorporated.

Turn the speed to medium-high and mix for 10 minutes. The dough should become smooth and elastic and be pulling away from the sides of the bowl. Turn the mixer speed to medium, add 2 tablespoons of the olive oil, and mix for 1–2 minutes. It will look like the olive oil is not going to mix into the dough, but give it time. Once it's incorporated, your dough will again be smooth and slightly glossy. Cover the stand mixer with a tea towel and leave the dough to rest for 10 minutes.

Using damp hands, pull the dough out of the mixer and place it onto an unfloured work surface. Use the slap and fold technique to strengthen the dough. Using slightly damp hands, pick up the far side of the dough, pull it up and toward your body, then slap it down and over the surface of the remaining dough that is sticking to the surface. Rotate the dough and repeat this for 2 minutes or until the dough is smooth. The dough will be very hydrated and will be difficult to handle, which is why it's important that your hands are damp and your surface is dry and can create friction.

Place 3 tablespoons of the olive oil in a large bowl. Add the dough to the bowl and rub the oil all over it to coat. Cover with plastic wrap or a clean kitchen towel and place in the fridge for 24–72 hours. The dough will double or even triple in size. This is the first rise.

1 (¼-oz/7 g) envelope active dry yeast

2⅔ cups (630 ml) lukewarm water (104°F)

1 teaspoon honey

5½ cups (700 g) bread flour

1 tablespoon fine sea salt

9 tablespoons (135 ml) extra-virgin olive oil, plus more for your hands

Flaky sea salt

Rosemary leaves

Recipe Continues →

continued from page 112

When you are ready to bake your focaccia, take the dough out of the fridge. Drizzle a 9 × 13 × 2-inch (23 × 33 × 5 cm) baking pan with 3 tablespoons of the olive oil, then gently place the dough in the pan. Gently stretch the dough out to the corners of the pan with your hands, making sure you don't use too much pressure as we don't want to deflate it too much. Don't worry if the dough does not stretch all the way out as it will double in size again. If there is any remaining olive oil in the bowl, pour it all over the dough.

For the second rise, cover the pan with a clean, damp kitchen towel or plastic wrap and place in a warm spot. Let rise for 2–4 hours. The dough will rise to the top of the pan.

Preheat the oven to 400°F.

Remove the kitchen towel or plastic wrap from the pan. Dampen your fingers with olive oil and press them into the dough to form dimples and release the gas. Bubbles will form and this is exactly what we are looking for! Sprinkle with sea salt flakes, rosemary leaves, and the remaining 1 tablespoon olive oil and bake for 30–35 minutes.

MAKES 1 LOAF

FOUR TOPPING IDEAS

¼ cup (70 g) Garlic Confit (page 16)

3 tablespoons Garlic Confit (page 16), ¼ cup (60 g) Cherry Tomato Confit (page 52), and 2¼ oz (60 g) buffalo mozzarella, torn

5–6 tablespoons (40–50 g) Olive Confit (page 62) or plain olives

3–4 tablespoons (45–60 g) Pesto Genovese (page 68) and a sprinkling of parmesan

Three focaccia sandwiches

ALL SERVE 1

THE ULTIMATE ITALIAN DELI SANDWICH

Make a roasted bell pepper spread by using a food processor to combine 3 Roasted Bell Peppers (page 64), 7 oz (200 g) crumbled feta, the juice of ½ lemon, 1½ tablespoons extra-virgin olive oil, and a pinch of salt and pepper. Cut a large piece of Focaccia (page 112) in half horizontally and spread a thick layer of the roasted bell pepper spread on one side. Spread a thick layer of Pesto Genovese (page 68) on the other. Top the roasted bell pepper spread with finely sliced prosciutto, salami, and olives, then finish with a thick layer of stracciatella cheese. Sprinkle with sun-dried tomatoes and top with the second bread slice.

STEAK SANDWICH WITH ROASTED GARLIC HERB BUTTER, GREEN HERB SAUCE & FRIES

Cook the Pan-Fried Steak (page 36) as directed in the recipe. Spoon 1½ tablespoons of Roasted Garlic Herb Butter (page 20) on top, let the steak rest for 5–10 minutes, then slice into strips. Cut a large piece of Focaccia (page 112) in half horizontally and spread a light layer of Olive Oil Mayo (page 54) on the bottom piece. Top with the steak slices and drizzle the butter all over. Place a large handful of french fries (page 102) on top and a light drizzle of Green Herb Sauce (page 83), then finish with the top piece of bread.

LEFTOVER ROASTED CHICKEN SANDWICH

Shred one leftover Olive Oil–Roasted Chicken breast (page 88) into a bowl. Mix in 1½ tablespoons of Olive Oil Mayo (page 54), ½ teaspoon Dijon mustard, ½ finely diced celery stalk, ¼ finely diced red onion, 2 teaspoons finely chopped pickle, and a handful each of finely chopped chives and parsley. Stir to combine and season to taste with salt and pepper. Butter two slices of Focaccia (page 112) and evenly distribute the chicken mixture over one slice. Top with some lettuce leaves and the top piece of bread. Cut in half and eat immediately.

New York bagels stole my heart. While I was visiting New York, I would begin every morning with an everything bagel slathered with cream cheese and topped with smoked salmon. I would hold my bagel wearing my thick gloves and walk down the freezing-cold New York streets, taking in the sights and sounds and feeling like a New Yorker. This bagel recipe is the closest I can get to this feeling while living on the other side of the world. Bagels do require a little skill, but don't let this deter you. The dough requires kneading and you need to know what to feel and look for, which comes with practice. There is also an art to the shaping, which is why I have offered the more traditional shaping method as well as a much easier way to do this. Both are great and won't alter your bagel experience in a dramatic way.

ALSO USED IN:

● *Citrus salmon bagel* *125*

Bagels

To make the everything bagel mix, combine all of the ingredients in a small jar and set aside.

In a small bowl, combine the water, yeast, and honey. Mix well and let rest for 5 minutes to activate the yeast. When bubbles form on the top of the water, the yeast is ready to use.

In a large bowl, combine the flour and salt. Add the yeast mixture to the flour and mix with a wooden spoon or your hands until blended. Lightly flour a work surface and scoop the dough onto it. Knead the dough for 10–15 minutes, until a stiff and smooth ball forms. Lightly dust the dough with more flour if any parts are too sticky.

Lightly drizzle a large bowl with olive oil and place the dough in it, seam side down. Cover with plastic wrap or a clean, damp kitchen towel and let rest for 2 hours in a warm spot. The dough will double in size.

Using your fist, punch the dough to deflate it and remove any air bubbles. Place the dough on an unfloured work surface. Using a sharp knife or dough cutter, divide the dough into 8 equal portions. They will weigh around 4 oz (110 g) each, so use a scale to measure them.

Form each piece of dough into a round by pinching the edges of the dough together and folding them over themselves. Place the dough rounds, seam side down, on an unfloured work surface and roll each into a ball by cupping your hand into a C-shape and rolling the dough back and forth. It's important this step be done on a work surface that has friction and has not been floured. Cover the dough balls with a clean, damp kitchen towel and let rest for 5 minutes.

EVERYTHING BAGEL MIX

3 tablespoons white sesame seeds

2 tablespoons black sesame seeds

2 tablespoons dried minced garlic

2 tablespoons dried minced onion

1 tablespoon black poppy seeds

1 teaspoon sea salt

BAGELS

1 cup plus 3 tablespoons (280 ml) lukewarm water (104°F)

1 (¼-oz/7 g) envelope active dry yeast

¼ cup (60 ml) honey or barley malt syrup, plus 2 tablespoons more for boiling

4 cups (500 g) bread flour, plus more for dusting

1¼ teaspoons sea salt flakes

Extra-virgin olive oil

Recipe Continues →

Line two baking sheets with parchment paper and very lightly brush with olive oil. There are two ways you can shape your bagels. The first is the more traditional way. Take one piece of dough and roll it out into a thick sausage shape. Apply extra pressure at the ends of the dough to slightly thin them. Wrap the dough around your hand with the ends overlapping each other. Pinch the ends together, then roll the dough back and forth on your work surface to form a closed circle shape. Apply pressure but not too much as you don't want to make this part of the bagel too thin. The hole in the middle should be 3 inches (7.5 cm) wide. Repeat this step to make 8 bagels. Place them on the prepared baking sheets, allowing enough space between each bagel (about three fingers) as they will expand in size.

The second way to shape the bagels is to place your thumb and an opposing finger in the middle of the dough ball and form a hole. Stretch out the dough with your fingers until the hole measures 3 inches (10 cm) across. This method is a lot easier!

Brush a piece of plastic wrap with olive oil and place it over the bagels. Cover with more plastic wrap and let rest in the fridge for 8–24 hours.

When you are ready to boil and bake the bagels, take them out of the fridge and bring to room temperature. Set up your bagel station by having a shallow bowl filled with the everything bagel mix, a wire rack for cooling, and a baking sheet lined with parchment paper at the ready.

Preheat the oven to 375°F.

Bring a saucepan of water to a boil and add the 2 tablespoons honey or barley malt syrup. If the water foams, scoop the foam off and discard. Lightly oil your hands (olive oil is a great hand moisturizer!) and pick up one bagel at a time. Place in the water and boil for 1 minute on each side, using a spatula to carefully flip them over. Boil the bagels in two or three batches. Place the bagels on the wire rack and let cool for 30–60 seconds. Dip the smooth side of the bagel into the bowl filled with the everything bagel mix—the topping will easily stick to the bagels.

Place on the prepared baking sheet, seed-side up, and bake for 20–25 minutes, until golden. You may need to rotate the baking sheet to ensure the bagels cook evenly.

Allow to cool on the wire rack, then serve with your choice of toppings (see page 124 for my favorite).

MAKES 8

TIP

Traditionally, barley malt syrup is used to give bagels their unique color and taste. In Australia, where I'm from, barley malt syrup is hard to come by, so I often make these bagels with honey, which works just as well!

Citrus
salmon bagel

Cut one bagel in half. Spread cream cheese over the bottom half and top with a large handful of leftover Salmon Confit with Citrus & Herbs (page 79). Sprinkle with some dill, capers, and finely sliced red onion. Top with the remaining bagel half.

SERVES 1

While this may look like a loaf of sourdough, it's actually the ultimate lazy loaf of bread. It requires no kneading, no starter, and basically no skill to make. If you're anything like me, you will have the biggest smile on your face when you pull this loaf out of the oven, because it looks and tastes like an artisan loaf that will set you back $10 at the latest trending bakery. All this recipe asks of you is to have a little time for it to rise and, ideally, a Dutch oven.

No-knead bread

1¼ cups (300 ml) luke-warm water (104°F)

1 (¼-oz/7 g) envelope active dry yeast

1 teaspoon honey

3¼ cups (400 g) bread flour, plus more for dusting

1¼ teaspoons fine sea salt

In a large bowl, combine the water, yeast, and honey. Mix well and let rest for 5 minutes to activate the yeast. When bubbles form on the top of the water, the yeast is ready to use.

In a large bowl, combine the flour and salt. Mix well. Add the yeast mixture to the bowl and mix with your hands or a wooden spoon until blended. The dough will be slightly sticky and shaggy. Cover with plastic wrap and let rest for 8–12 hours in a warm spot or 24 hours in the fridge. The dough will double in size and bubbles will form on top.

Place the dough on a lightly floured work surface. Fold the dough over itself at least six times. Flip the dough over so it is seam side down and shape into a ball with your hands. Cover with the bowl or a clean, damp kitchen towel and let rest on a piece of parchment paper for 1–2 hours.

In the final 45 minutes of resting, preheat the oven to 425°F. While the oven is warming, place an enameled cast-iron Dutch oven into it.

After 45 minutes, take the hot pot out of the oven. Using a sharp knife or bread scorer, score either the left or right top side of the bread, just off-center, roughly 1 inch (2.5 cm) deep. Use the parchment paper to carefully lift the dough into the hot Dutch oven.

Cover with the lid and bake for 30 minutes. Remove the lid and bake for 15 minutes more or until the top is golden and crunchy.

Let cool on a wire rack for 30 minutes before slicing.

MAKES 1 LOAF

Four toast toppers

ALL SERVE 1

PEACH, GARLIC CONFIT & BURRATA

Drizzle one side of a slice of No-Knead Bread (page 127) with extra-virgin olive oil and place in a cast-iron skillet. Cook over very low heat for roughly 10 minutes on each side or until golden and crispy. Slice and grill 1 peach (page 61). Spread up to 4 cloves of Garlic Confit (page 16) on the bread. Place one 4½ oz (125 g) burrata ball on top, cut it open, and spread it out over the bread. Place the peach on top of the burrata and drizzle with balsamic glaze. Finish with a sprinkling of finely sliced red onion and some basil leaves.

AVOCADO WITH CURED EGG YOLK

Drizzle one side of a slice of No-Knead Bread (page 127) with extra-virgin olive oil and place in a cast-iron skillet. Cook over very low heat for roughly 10 minutes on each side or until golden and crispy. Using a sharp knife, cut 1 avocado in half and remove the pit. (If only making one serving, save the other half for another use.) Cut the nose off the avocado, then place your finger between the flesh and skin of the avocado and very gently peel back the skin. Slice the avocado diagonally, creating slices ⅓ inch (1 cm) thick. Gently push the avocado slices away from one another to fan them out. Place a spatula or flat tool, such as a large knife, under the avocado and transfer it to your piece of olive oil–fried bread. Using a microplane, grate 1 Cured Egg Yolk (page 155) over the avocado and season with salt and pepper and an extra drizzle of olive oil, plus some chile flakes, if desired.

TOMATO & PESTO

Drizzle one side of a slice of No-Knead Bread (page 127) with extra-virgin olive oil and place in a cast-iron skillet. Cook over very low heat for roughly 10 minutes on each side or until golden and crispy. Rub a piece of raw garlic over the bread. Smear a light layer of stracciatella cheese over the bread, followed by 1½ tablespoons Pesto Genovese (page 68). Top with 2–4 tomato slices. Season the tomato with Garlic Chip Seasoning (page 159). Finish with slices of freshly shaved prosciutto.

CAESAR SALAD WITH BREADED CHICKEN & CARAMELIZED ONIONS

Drizzle one side of a slice of No-Knead Bread (page 127) with extra-virgin olive oil and place in a cast-iron skillet. Cook over very low heat for roughly 10 minutes on each side or until golden and crispy. Place a large handful of Caesar Salad (page 150) on the bread. Top with slices of Crispy Breaded Chicken (page 145) and a spoonful of Caramelized Onions (page 80).

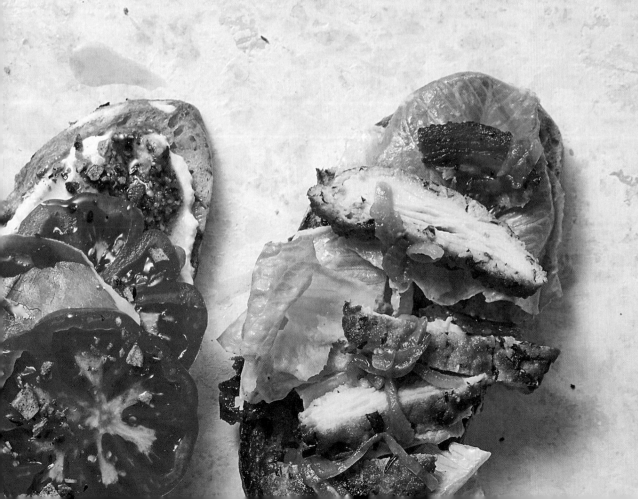

5

Crumbs

Mum's famous breadcrumbs
Popcorn eggplant
Abuelo's egg croquettes
Nanna's broccoli pasta with cured egg yolk breadcrumbs
Mac 'n' cheese with breadcrumbs
Crispy breaded chicken
Chicken parm
Garlic butter stuffed chicken
Caesar salad with bacon fat croutons

These breadcrumbs have affectionately become known as "Mum's famous breadcrumbs" because of how often my mum and I use them in our cooking. Case in point, they are used in all but one of the recipes in this chapter. They are versatile, simple, and just downright delicious. So why am I asking you to drag out your food processor to make something that can easily be purchased from the supermarket? Because you can't even compare the two! Store-bought breadcrumbs are usually blended so finely that they resemble more of a powder than a crumb, and will result in a soggy mess as soon as they touch your pan. Mum's famous breadcrumbs are full of fresh herbs offering a lovely green color, and are blended to a chunky texture that makes every bite taste and feel like a mini crouton. You can make a large batch and store them in a jar in your pantry or in ziplock bags in your freezer for several months.

Mum's famous breadcrumbs

If the bread is fresh, lay the slices on a baking sheet or wire rack and let dry out overnight or for a minimum of 4 hours. For a quicker option, you can lightly toast the bread in a toaster and allow to cool before using.

Roughly tear the bread apart and place in a food processor with the parsley and rosemary. Blend until the bread is still quite chunky and the herbs are mixed in. We aren't looking for a fine and crumbly texture as it's those chunky, crusty parts that make these breadcrumbs extra special. If you are using a small blender, you will need to do this in batches. Place the breadcrumbs in a large bowl or an airtight container and store in the pantry or fridge for 4 days or freezer for 3 months.

MAKES 10 CUPS (750 G)

1 loaf sliced white sandwich bread (about 1 lb 9 oz/700 g)

1 small bunch of flat-leaf parsley (about 1½ oz/40 g), leaves and stems

2 rosemary sprigs, leaves picked and finely chopped

TIPS

For the best breadcrumbs, I recommend buying a cheap loaf of white sandwich bread. I have tried every type of bread and this makes the best crumbs! You can also mix in any leftover No-Knead Bread (page 127).

It's important the bread you are using is not fresh and is a few days old. Fresh bread will be too moist, resulting in a breadcrumb that doesn't stick to your protein or veg. If using fresh bread, you can either dry it out the day before or pop in the toaster and allow to cool before making your breadcrumbs. Be sure to use the crusts of the bread when making your breadcrumbs as they create the crispiest layer.

I remember the utter delight I felt when KFC released their popcorn chicken. I thought it was one of the most amazing bite-sized snacks I could munch on in the back of the car as Mum drove me home from school. Because I became a little too obsessed with them, requesting a box every ride home, my mum challenged herself to make a healthier homemade version. This is how our popcorn eggplant came to be invented. It's little pieces of pure crispy heaven and, of course, Mum's famous breadcrumbs have been used to achieve that beautiful chunky crumb.

Popcorn eggplant

2 eggs

2 garlic cloves, minced

1 eggplant

Sea salt

1⅓ cups (100 g) Mum's Famous Breadcrumbs (page 132)

6 tablespoons (45 g) grated Pecorino Romano, plus more for serving

¼ cup (35 g) all-purpose flour

Freshly ground black pepper

Light olive oil, for frying

1 cup (240 ml) Tomato & Basil Sauce (page 55), for serving

In a wide shallow bowl, whisk together the eggs and garlic and set aside. By preparing this early, the garlic will have time to release its flavor into the egg.

Trim the ends off the eggplant and cut the eggplant into discs 1½ inches (4 cm) thick. Stack the discs on top of each other, then slice into ¾-inch (2 cm) cubes.

Place the eggplant in a colander and very generously salt it with sea salt. Let sit over the sink or on paper towels for 45 minutes, to allow as much moisture as possible to be released.

Press down firmly on the eggplant to remove any last moisture, then rinse under cold water to remove the salt. Transfer to a plate or wooden board lined with paper towels. Pat the eggplant dry with paper towels.

In a shallow bowl, mix together the breadcrumbs and Pecorino Romano.

In a wide shallow bowl, whisk together the flour with a generous amount of salt and pepper. Set up a dredging station. Have the shallow bowl with the flour, then the bowl with the beaten eggs, followed by a plate with the bread-crumbs, and finally a large clean plate or baking sheet to place the crumbed eggplant on.

Working with a handful of eggplant cubes at a time, roll them around in the flour until they are evenly coated. Dip them in the eggs and then the breadcrumbs—apply pressure with the hand you are using for dry ingredients to coat the eggplant with the crumbs. Transfer to the clean plate and repeat with the remaining eggplant.

Fill a large skillet with a generous amount of olive oil—about 1 inch (2.5 cm) deep. Heat the olive oil over high heat until bubbles form around a wooden skewer inserted upright in the pan. Decrease the heat to medium-low and fry one handful of eggplant at a time for 4 minutes on each side, or until golden and crispy. Transfer to a wire rack with paper towels placed underneath.

Sprinkle the eggplant with a generous amount of Pecorino Romano and serve with the tomato and basil sauce.

SERVES 4

TIP
When crumbing, use one hand for dry ingredients and one hand for wet!

While I was writing this book, my mum became very unwell. While I spent weeks consumed with worry about her, my mind also drifted to thinking about this croquette recipe. It's a long-standing family recipe passed down from my abuelo. There were countless times in my teenage years when Mum would call me over to the kitchen to join in with her, my nanna, and my brother as they mixed the roux and rolled the croquettes through her famous breadcrumbs, but I was far more interested in chatting with my friends and would shout, "Next time!" But that's the thing about life. You always think you have all the time in the world to ask those you love all the questions you have wanted answers to, but life can change in an instant. I'm very happy to report that my mum is doing so much better now, but for a very long time she wasn't. So, through Zoom calls and many back-and-forth texts with my brother, I taught myself how to make our family egg croquettes. I was able to freeze a few and cook them up for my mum when she was feeling up to it, and her exact words were, "Yep, that's them."

Abuelo's egg croquettes

Ice water

6 eggs

7 tablespoons (100 ml) extra-virgin olive oil

5 garlic cloves, minced

1 cup plus 2 tablespoons (140 g) all-purpose flour

2 cups (480 ml) whole milk

Sea salt

Freshly ground black pepper

CRUMB

4 eggs

4 garlic cloves, minced

2⅔–5⅓ cups (200–400 g) Mum's Famous Breadcrumbs (page 132)

Light olive oil, for frying

Bring a saucepan of water to a boil. Meanwhile, fill a bowl with ice and water. Decrease the heat under the saucepan to medium so the water is slowly simmering. Carefully add the eggs and cook for 12 minutes, then place them in the ice bath for 10 minutes. This will prevent the eggs from cooking any further and allow them to cool slightly so they are easy to peel.

Peel the eggs and place them in a bowl. Mash with a fork or potato masher until you have a fine and crumbly texture. Set aside.

Heat the extra-virgin olive oil in a large, deep nonstick skillet over medium-low heat and fry the garlic for 2 minutes or until slightly fragrant. It's very important that the garlic does not burn or brown.

Increase the heat to medium and add the flour. Stir it in for 2–3 minutes, until you have a gritty roux.

Add the milk, ½ cup (120 ml) at a time, to the roux and mix well after each addition until fully incorporated. You will need to stir quite vigorously as the roux begins to thicken up, so brace yourself for an arm workout! The roux will start to form a ball and be quite soft in texture.

Take the pan off the heat, and stir in the egg, along with a generous amount of salt and pepper. Taste the mixture and adjust to your preference.

Spoon the mixture onto a large plate (you may need two plates) and flatten it out until it's ¾ inch (2 cm) thick. Cover and place in the fridge to chill for a minimum of 2 hours but ideally overnight.

Recipe Continues →

For the crumb, in a wide shallow bowl, whisk together the eggs and garlic and set aside.

Set up a dredging station. Have a plate with the breadcrumbs, then a bowl with the beaten eggs, and finally a large clean plate or baking sheet to place the croquettes on.

Take roughly 1½ tablespoons of the egg mixture in your hands and roll it into a fat cigar shape about 2½ inches (6 cm) long. Cup this shape firmly in your hands to mold it into a croquette.

Roll the croquette in the breadcrumbs, then in the beaten eggs, ensuring it's evenly coated. Roll it in the breadcrumbs a second time, then transfer to the clean plate. Repeat with the remaining mixture.

Fill a large skillet over high heat with a generous amount of light olive oil—about 1 inch (2.5 cm) deep. Heat the olive oil until bubbles form around a wooden skewer inserted upright in the pan. Decrease the heat to medium-low and fry 3–4 croquettes at a time for 4 minutes on each side or until golden and crispy. Transfer to a wire rack.

Serve immediately.

MAKES ABOUT 16

The aroma of pasta, chicken stock, and broccoli bubbling away together always brings on a sense of nostalgia for when my brother and I would eat this meal in my nanna's tiny brown-brick apartment. My version is slightly different from my nanna's, because she wasn't the type to cure an egg yolk. However, she would sprinkle some of our famous breadcrumbs, which were cooked with anchovy, over the top of the pasta for that lovely crunchy and salty element. Cured egg yolks have that sharp and salty umami flavor that is also found in anchovies or Pecorino Romano. This is a great midweek meal that can be thrown together so quickly. The breadcrumbs are optional but highly recommended.

Nanna's broccoli pasta with cured egg yolk breadcrumbs

¼ cup (60 ml) plus
   1½ tablespoons
   extra-virgin olive oil

2 garlic cloves, minced

1 teaspoon ground white pepper

3¼ cups (750 ml) chicken stock

Sea salt

10 oz (300 g) small pasta shells

1 head of broccoli (about
   10 oz/300 g), cut into
   small pieces

2 tablespoons grated
   Pecorino Romano

1⅓ cups (100 g) Mum's Famous
   Breadcrumbs (page 132)

¼ teaspoon chile flakes

1 Cured Egg Yolk (page 155)

In an enameled cast-iron Dutch oven over high heat, combine ¼ cup (60 ml) of the olive oil, the garlic, white pepper, chicken stock, and a pinch of salt. Bring to a boil.

Once the water is boiling, decrease the heat to medium, add the pasta and broccoli to the pan, and stir well. Stirring occasionally, keep the water at a rapid boil for 15 minutes or until 80 percent of the stock has evaporated and the pasta is cooked. Decrease the heat to low, add the Pecorino Romano, and stir it in until you have a smooth and silky texture.

While the pasta is cooking, heat the remaining 1½ tablespoons olive oil in a small saucepan over medium heat. Add the breadcrumbs and stir them into the oil for 5 minutes, or until golden and crispy. Remove the pan from the heat, sprinkle in the chile flakes, and grate in the cured egg yolk. Stir well.

Sprinkle the breadcrumb mixture over the pasta and serve immediately.

SERVES 4

My partner, Joel, has minimal cooking skills, which had never been a problem in our house since I love to cook and he returns the favor by washing up all the dishes. We had a great routine in place. That was, until I became pregnant with our first daughter and my feet were so swollen that I could only stand on them for a minute at a time. Being the thoughtful partner that he is, Joel went out and bought an outdoor grill. He felt confident that he could grill a steak or a whole chicken that I had marinated the day before. From this, his passion for grilling and mine for finding the perfect side dishes to his grilled meat began. I reached out to my friend Rachael from the American South for advice on how to make the best mac 'n' cheese, and she directed me to a recipe by chef Ashley Christensen. Surprisingly to me, it used no roux. It was just cream and cheese, and one of the best mac 'n' cheeses I had ever eaten! I have tinkered with this recipe to make it my own, but it is heavily influenced by Ashley's recipe.

SERVE WITH:

- *Pan-fried steak with aglio e olio sauce* *36*
- *Simple salad with lemon & honey vinaigrette* *57*

Mac 'n' cheese with breadcrumbs

Preheat the oven to 350°F.

In a large pot of heavily salted boiling water, cook the pasta for about 5 minutes, until barely al dente. Drain.

While the pasta is cooking, bring the cream and a pinch of salt to a simmer in a saucepan over low heat. Simmer for 5 minutes to slightly thicken the cream, stirring often. Add the pasta to the pan with the cream and stir well for 2 minutes. Add the cheeses, one-third at a time, stirring after each addition, until fully melted and you have a smooth texture.

Place the breadcrumbs, olive oil, and a generous amount of salt in a small skillet over medium heat. Fry for several minutes or until golden.

Transfer the mac 'n' cheese to an 8 × 10-inch (20 × 25 cm) baking dish (or multiple small dishes) and sprinkle the breadcrumbs over the top. Bake for 15 minutes, then serve immediately.

SERVES 4

Sea salt

9 oz (250 g) elbow macaroni or small pasta shells

2½ cups (600 ml) heavy cream

½ cup (50 g) shredded Jarlsberg

6 tablespoons (50 g) grated Pecorino Romano or parmesan

1⅓ cups (150 g) shredded cheddar

⅔ cup (50 g) Mum's Famous Breadcrumbs (page 132)

2½ tablespoons extra-virgin olive oil

This was my first video to ever go viral and was really the recipe that changed everything for me. It turned Daen's Kitchen from a hobby and into a career. I began the video with the line, "I'm going to share my mum's secrets on how to make the crispiest and best crumbed chicken." And that's exactly what I am going to do for you again here. First, we must use Mum's famous breadcrumbs for that superior crust. Second, we add garlic to the beaten eggs for a lovely subtle garlic flavor throughout. And third, we fry the chicken in a light olive oil for not only a gorgeous golden color, but also a little extra flavor.

SERVE WITH:

Grilled peach, tomato & burrata salad with basil olive oil 61

ALSO USED IN:

Caesar salad with crumbed chicken & caramelized onions (on toast) 129

Chicken parm 146

Crispy breaded chicken

4 eggs

4 garlic cloves, minced

4½ lb (2 kg) boneless, skinless chicken breasts

10 cups (750 g) Mum's Famous Breadcrumbs (page 132)

1 cup plus 3 tablespoons (150 g) all-purpose flour

1 teaspoon sea salt

1 teaspoon freshly ground black pepper

Light olive oil, for frying

In a wide shallow bowl, whisk together the eggs and garlic and set aside to allow the garlic to release its flavor into the egg.

Using a sharp knife, cut through the middle of each chicken breast, horizontally. Let the knife do most of the work, applying a small amount of pressure as the knife glides through crosswise. It's easiest when you place one hand on top of the chicken breast. Repeat this step with the remaining chicken breasts.

Place one piece of chicken between two pieces of plastic wrap. Using the smooth side of a meat mallet, pound the chicken from the center outward until the breast is roughly ¾ inch (2 cm) thick and has an even thickness throughout. This step is to ensure the chicken cooks evenly. Set aside.

Place the breadcrumbs in a large bowl.

In a wide shallow bowl, whisk together the flour, salt, and pepper, then set up your dredging station. Begin with a plate of the flour, followed by the beaten eggs, followed by the breadcrumbs, and finish with a large clean plate or baking sheet to place the crumbed chicken on.

Take one chicken breast and coat both sides evenly in the flour, then place in the egg wash and coat both sides evenly. Lastly, place in the breadcrumb mixture, applying pressure with your hands when you flip the chicken over to ensure the breadcrumbs are evenly adhered all over. Transfer the chicken to the clean plate, then repeat with the remaining chicken. Place the plate of chicken in the fridge for 15 minutes to allow the crumbs to set.

Fill a large skillet with a generous amount of olive oil—about 1 inch (2.5 cm) deep. Heat the olive oil over high heat until bubbles form around a wooden skewer placed upright in the pan. Decrease the heat to medium-low and fry one or two pieces of chicken at a time for 2–3 minutes on each side, until golden and crispy. It's best to test one piece of chicken to make sure your cook time and heat levels are accurate. Transfer the cooked chicken to a wire rack with paper towels underneath and let rest for 5 minutes, then serve.

SERVES 12

TIP

This makes a large batch of breaded chicken, so you can store it in the freezer, uncooked, and always have it on hand!

Chicken parm is my partner's absolute favorite meal. So much so, that when you ask him what his death row meal would be, he responds with chicken parm. With cooking and food being my love language, I was determined to create the best chicken parm known to man, which I believe I have achieved. I'm able to state this confidently because Joel tells me it's the best chicken parm he's ever eaten every time I make it for him. And he definitely wouldn't be stretching the truth just because I am his partner, of course. This recipe is a great way to use up my crispy crumbed chicken and tomato and basil sauce.

Chicken parm

Halve, pound, and coat the chicken breasts as directed for the Crispy Breaded Chicken, but do not cook.

Preheat the oven to 400°F. Place a cast-iron skillet in the oven so it's piping hot when you are ready to assemble your chicken parm. This step is very important as it will ensure your chicken stays crispy on the bottom.

Fill a large skillet with a generous amount of olive oil—about 1 inch (2.5 cm) deep. Heat the olive oil over high heat until bubbles form around a wooden skewer inserted upright in the pan. Decrease the heat to medium-low and fry the chicken for 2–3 minutes on each side, until golden and crispy. It's best to test one piece of chicken to make sure your cook time and heat levels are accurate. Transfer the cooked chicken to a wire rack with paper towels underneath and let rest for 5 minutes.

Take the cast-iron pan out of the oven. Change the oven setting to broil.

Very carefully place the chicken in the hot cast-iron pan. Generously spoon the tomato and basil sauce on top to cover most of the chicken. Cover with the parmesan, then the mozzarella. Place under the broiler for 4 minutes, or until the cheese has melted and is bubbling. Allow to slightly cool, then scatter with basil leaves, if desired, and serve.

SERVES 2

2 pieces of Crispy Crumbed Chicken (page 145), uncooked

Light olive oil, for frying

½–⅔ cup (120–160 ml) Tomato & Basil Sauce (page 55)

6 tablespoons (50 g) grated parmesan

4½ oz (125 g) mozzarella, cut into discs 1½ inches (4 cm) thick

Basil leaves (optional)

I feel like stuffed chicken breast is making a comeback. This is a very contemporary take on a more traditional Chicken Kiev. I have stuffed the chicken with my roasted garlic herb butter, lots of cheese, and slices of ham. Take a moment to enjoy the butter oozing out when you cut into this one.

Garlic butter stuffed chicken

4 large boneless, skinless chicken breasts (8 oz/225 g each)

Sea salt

Freshly ground black pepper

4 thin slices ham

4 slices (¾–1 oz/25–30 g total) cold Roasted Garlic Herb Butter (page 20)

⅔ cup (70 g) shredded mozzarella

1 cup plus 3 tablespoons (150 g) all-purpose flour, plus more for dusting

3 eggs

2 garlic cloves, minced

4 cups (300 g) Mum's Famous Breadcrumbs (page 132)

3 cups (720 ml) light olive oil, for shallow-frying

Make a horizontal cut through the center of each chicken breast lengthwise, ensuring you don't cut all the way through in order to keep the chicken breast intact. Spread the chicken breast open and place it between two pieces of plastic wrap. Using the smooth side of a mallet, pound the chicken to 1 inch (2.5 cm) thick, making sure you do not make any holes in the chicken. Set aside and repeat with the remaining chicken breasts.

Line a work surface, such as a cutting board, with plastic wrap. Place the chicken breasts on the board and season with salt and pepper. Layer each breast with a slice of ham and a slice of the roasted garlic herb butter, then sprinkle with one-quarter of the mozzarella. Dust the edges of each chicken breast with flour as this will help it stick together, then roll each chicken breast up tightly. Now roll the chicken in plastic wrap, twisting the ends of the plastic wrap so the chicken is tightly enclosed. Place on a clean plate and pop in the fridge for 2 hours.

In a wide shallow bowl, whisk together the eggs and garlic and set aside. Preparing this early allows the garlic to release its flavor into the eggs.

Set up a dredging station in three wide shallow bowls: In one bowl, whisk together the flour and a pinch each of salt and pepper. Set the bowl of eggs next to the flour. Follow with a third bowl with the breadcrumbs. Finish with a large clean plate or baking sheet to place the crumbed chicken on.

Remove the plastic wrap from the chicken. Coat all sides of one piece of chicken in the flour, followed by the beaten egg and finally the breadcrumbs—apply pressure with your hands to ensure the breadcrumbs stick. Place the crumbed chicken on the prepared clean plate and repeat with the remaining chicken. Place in the fridge for 30 minutes to allow the breadcrumbs to set.

Preheat the oven to 350°F. Set a wire rack in a sheet pan.

Heat the oil in a deep saucepan. Check if the oil is hot enough by placing an upright wooden skewer in the pan and seeing if bubbles form around it. Decrease the heat to medium-low and fry the chicken for 1–2 minutes on each side, until golden and crispy. Spoon the hot oil over the chicken while the underside is cooking. Transfer to the wire rack in the sheet pan and bake for 15–17 minutes, until the internal temperature of the chicken is 165°F (74°C).

Serve immediately.

SERVES 4

There are moments in life that will stay with you forever, and one of those moments, for me, was when my friend's mum introduced me to bacon fat–fried bread. Not to be dramatic, but bacon fat–fried bread changed my life. It's salty, rich, smoky, and so wrong that it's right. As this Caesar salad calls for lots of bacon, it was the perfect opportunity to share my love for bacon fat–fried bread. The fatty croutons add such depth of flavor to an already flavorful meal. I love to serve this salad with some breaded chicken (page 145) and caramelized onions (page 80) on the side. Go hard or go home.

Caesar salad with bacon fat croutons

To make the bacon fat croutons, preheat the oven to 400°F. Line a baking sheet with parchment paper.

Place the bacon in a large cold skillet. Turn the heat to high and cook the bacon until crispy. Remove the bacon from the pan, reserving all of the fat.

In a large bowl, toss the bread with all of the bacon fat and a drizzle of olive oil, until evenly coated. Place on the lined baking sheet. Bake in the oven for 12 minutes, or until golden and crispy, rotating the baking sheet front to back halfway through if needed. Season with salt.

To make the salad dressing, in a food processor, blend the garlic and anchovy fillets until smooth. Add the Worcestershire sauce, mustard, egg yolk, and lemon juice. Blend while slowly pouring in the olive oil until emulsified and smooth. Stir in the parmesan and season with a pinch of salt and pepper.

To make the salad, bring a saucepan of water to a boil. Meanwhile, set up a large bowl of ice and water. Decrease the heat under the saucepan to medium so the water is slowly simmering. Carefully add the eggs and cook for 12 minutes, then place them in the ice bath for 10 minutes. This will prevent the eggs from cooking any further and allow them to cool slightly so they are easy to peel. Peel the eggs and cut into quarters.

In a large bowl, toss the lettuce and dressing until the lettuce is evenly coated. Add the bacon and toss to combine. Scatter the croutons and egg quarters on top and finish with a sprinkling of parmesan.

SERVES 6

BACON FAT CROUTONS

10½ oz (300 g) bacon, diced

4 slices No-Knead Bread (page 127), torn into small squares

Extra-virgin olive oil, for drizzling

Sea salt

SALAD DRESSING

1 garlic clove, peeled but whole

4 anchovy fillets

1 teaspoon Worcestershire sauce

1 teaspoon Dijon mustard

1 egg yolk, at room temperature

2 tablespoons lemon juice

½ cup (120 ml) extra-virgin olive oil

¼ cup (25 g) grated parmesan

Sea salt

Freshly ground black pepper

SALAD

4 eggs, fridge-cold

Ice water

2 romaine lettuce hearts, chopped

Grated parmesan, for serving

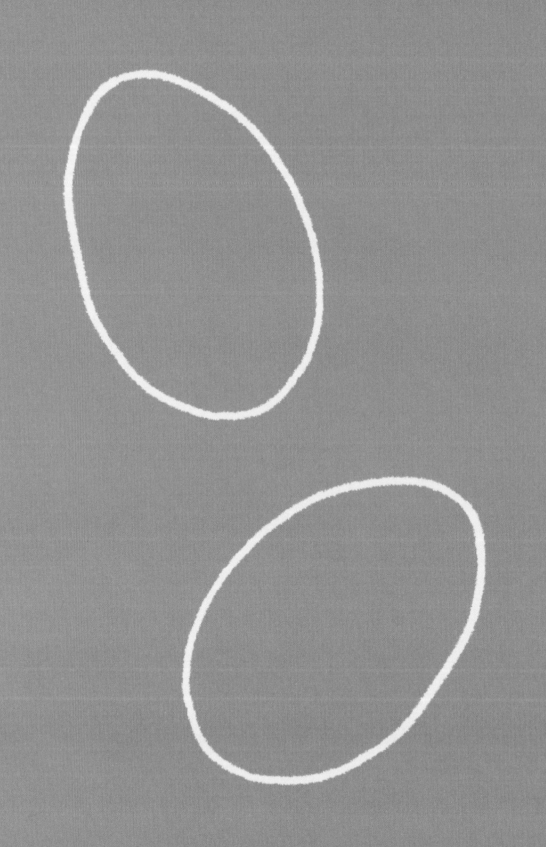

6

Eggs

Cured egg yolk
Chorizo fat–fried eggs with crispy potatoes
Jammy eggs with garlic chip seasoning
Spinach, feta & pine nut quiche
Creamy egg salad
Italian egg drop soup (stracciatella)
Egg pasta dough

How incredibly amazing are cured egg yolks? While they may look like dried apricots, or even some sort of orange candy, they are actually salt-cured, dehydrated egg yolks. The salt draws out the moisture from the egg yolks and makes them hard enough to be grated, sliced, or shaved. They have a salty and rich flavor that tastes a little like sharp parmesan and can be used as a topping on your pastas, pizzas, or even avocado toast.

ALSO USED IN:

● *Avocado with cured egg yolk (on toast)* *128*

◖ *Nanna's broccoli pasta with cured egg yolk breadcrumbs* *141*

Cured egg yolk

About 2 cups (500 g) fine sea salt
6 egg yolks

Pour a layer of fine sea salt ¾–1½ inches (2–4 cm) thick into an 8 × 6-inch (20 × 15 cm) glass baking dish.

Use the rounded back of a 1-tablespoon measuring spoon to create 6 indents in the salt, evenly spaced apart.

Carefully drop the egg yolks into the indents and completely cover them with salt. You should not be able to see any of the yolk. Cover and place in the fridge for 6–7 days.

Preheat the oven to 200°F or the lowest possible setting.

Carefully remove the egg yolks from the salt mixture with your hands and rinse under cold water to remove the excess salt. Pat dry with paper towels and place on a wire rack lined with parchment paper set over a baking sheet.

Bake for 1 hour or until the egg yolks have dehydrated and are dry to the touch.

Store in an airtight container in the fridge for up to 1 month.

MAKES 6

TIP
To double the recipe, you will need a 12 × 8-inch (30 × 20 cm) glass dish. Adjust the salt quantity as needed to cover the egg yolks by the ¾–1½ inches (2–4 cm) called for.

My uncle told me that when he eats this dish, he feels extremely Spanish. That's because this is quite a traditional Spanish dish, best served with a piece of crusty white bread to mop up the runny egg yolk and chorizo fat. My abuelo would eat this breakfast most weekend mornings, with a side of roasted bell peppers. I encourage you to do the same!

Chorizo fat–fried eggs with crispy potatoes

Heat the olive oil in a small to medium skillet over high heat. Add half the potatoes to the hot oil and season with salt and pepper. Fry for 1–2 minutes on each side, until golden and crispy. Remove the potatoes from the pan with a slotted spoon, reserving the oil in the pan, and transfer to a wire rack set over paper towels. Repeat with the remaining potatoes.

In the same skillet over medium-high heat, cook the chorizo in the reserved oil for 2–3 minutes on each side, until crispy and slightly charred. Remove from the pan with a slotted spoon, ensuring all the fat and oil is left behind.

Crack the eggs into the same skillet over high heat. Fry until the edges are golden and crispy and the whites are puffed and bubbly. Tilt the pan on an angle and scoop up the oil with a spoon to baste over the whites to ensure they are fully cooked. Remove the eggs from the pan with a spatula and set aside.

Place each egg on a piece of toasted bread and top with a sprinkling of parsley. Serve with the sliced roasted bell pepper, potatoes, and the chorizo on the side.

SERVES 2

¼ cup (60 ml) extra-virgin olive oil

2 small baby potatoes, very finely sliced

Sea salt

Freshly ground black pepper

9 oz (250 g) Spanish-style chorizo, cut into thick slices

2 eggs

2 slices No-Knead Bread (page 127), toasted

Large handful of flat-leaf parsley leaves, finely chopped

1 Roasted Bell Pepper (page 64), sliced

If I could only eat one type of egg for the rest of my life, it would be a jammy egg. The yolk is luxuriously spoonable and sits in that sweet spot between runny and hard-boiled. It's the ideal consistency. Eating them on their own is pretty delicious, but sprinkling the garlic chip seasoning over them with a dash of white vinegar is a great move.

Jammy eggs with garlic chip seasoning

GARLIC CHIP SEASONING

1 teaspoon fennel seeds

½ teaspoon Aleppo pepper

2½ tablespoons Garlic Chips (page 20)

1 tablespoon onion flakes

Pinch of sea salt

JAMMY EGGS

2 eggs, fridge-cold

Ice water

½ cucumber, finely sliced

¼ red onion, finely sliced

1 teaspoon lemon juice

1 tablespoon garlic oil (reserved oil from the Garlic Chips; see page 20)

Large handful of dill fronds, chopped

⅓–½ cup (90–130 g) Greek yogurt

Splash of distilled white vinegar

2 slices No-Knead Bread (page 127), lightly fried in olive oil until golden

To make the garlic chip seasoning, toast the fennel seeds in a dry skillet over medium heat for 1–2 minutes. Remove from the pan and place in a mortar with the Aleppo pepper. Using the pestle, blend until fine.

Add the garlic chips, onion flakes, and salt to the mortar and grind until you have a chunky texture.

To make the jammy eggs, bring a saucepan of water to a boil. Meanwhile, set up a bowl of ice and water. Decrease the heat under the saucepan to medium so the water is at a slow simmer. Add the eggs and cook for 7½ minutes, then place in the ice bath for 10 minutes. This will prevent the eggs from cooking any further and allow them to cool slightly so they are easy to peel. Peel the eggs and cut them in half.

While the eggs are boiling, salt the cucumbers and leave to sit. Drain the excess liquid from the bowl.

In the same bowl with the cucumbers, combine the onion, lemon juice, and garlic oil and mix until combined. Sprinkle with the dill.

Divide the Greek yogurt between plates and place the cucumber salad and jammy eggs on top. Season the eggs with a tiny splash of vinegar and a large pinch of the garlic chip seasoning. Serve with the olive oil–fried bread.

SERVES 2

Who doesn't love a quiche? It's a great dish that will offer lots of leftovers for meals throughout the week. I have used my garlic confit and sour cream puff pastry, but you can easily use a store-bought puff pastry if you are short on time.

Spinach, feta & pine nut quiche

On a floured work surface, use a rolling pin to roll the pastry into a round that is 12 inches (30 cm) in diameter. Roll the pastry onto your rolling pin and carefully lay it over a 9-inch (23 cm) pie dish. Press it into the dish with your fingers, ensuring it's completely smooth. Clean up the edges of the pastry by cutting off the uneven bits—however, be very careful to leave at least ¾–1½ inches (2–4 cm) of overhanging pastry. Fold the overhanging pastry back over the edges of the pie dish and crimp it with your fingers. Line the pastry with parchment paper and fill evenly with pie weights or uncooked rice. Place in the fridge to chill for 30 minutes.

Preheat the oven to 375°F. Partially blind bake the crust for 15 minutes. Take the crust out of the oven and remove the parchment paper and pie weights or rice. Prick the bottom of the crust with a fork six times. Return to the oven and bake for 7 minutes, or until golden and crispy. Set aside to cool slightly.

Leave the oven on and decrease the temperature to 350°F. Meanwhile, place the spinach into a bowl sprinkle with 2 teaspoons of salt. Leave to sit for 15 minutes to allow the spinach to sweat and release excess water. Place the spinach into a cheesecloth or fine tea towel and squeeze out as much water as you can from the spinach. Roughly chop and set aside.

In a large dry skillet, toast the pine nuts over medium-low heat for several minutes, or until golden and toasty. Set aside.

Heat the olive oil in the same skillet over medium-low heat. Fry the onion and garlic for 5 minutes, or until fragrant and translucent, stirring occasionally to prevent the garlic from burning. Remove from the heat, add the spinach and pine nuts, and stir them in.

In a large bowl, whisk together the eggs, milk, and heavy cream. Season with salt and pepper.

Spoon the garlic, onion, spinach, and pine nut mixture into the partially baked quiche crust. Crumble the feta over the top and sprinkle with the Gruyère and parmesan. Pour in the egg mixture and bake for 35–40 minutes, until golden on top. The middle should be firm yet still have a slight jiggle to it. Let rest for 10 minutes before serving.

SERVES 4

All-purpose flour, for dusting

½ recipe Garlic Confit & Sour Cream Puff Pastry (page 23)

3.5 oz (100 g) baby spinach

Sea salt

⅓ cup (50 g) pine nuts

¼ cup (60 ml) extra-virgin olive oil

1 onion, finely diced

4 garlic cloves, minced

4 eggs

⅔ cup (160 ml) whole milk

⅔ cup (160 ml) heavy cream

Freshly ground black pepper

2½ oz (75 g) Greek feta, crumbled

½ cup (50 g) grated Gruyère

6 tablespoons (50 g) grated parmesan

This is the best egg salad you will ever eat. What makes it stand out from others is what I like to call the egg yolk dressing. This is made by separating the yolks from the whites and mixing them into mayonnaise and Dijon mustard until smooth. Egg salad is extremely quick to whip up and a great dish to have stored in the fridge to slowly eat throughout the week.

Creamy egg salad

Ice water

6 eggs

2½ tablespoons mayonnaise, store-bought or homemade (page 54)

1 teaspoon Dijon mustard

1 tablespoon lemon juice

2 teaspoons extra-virgin olive oil

Pinch of sea salt

Pinch of freshly ground black pepper

4 slices No-Knead Bread (page 127), toasted

1 avocado, sliced (optional)

Snipped chives (optional)

Bring a saucepan of water to a boil. Meanwhile, fill a bowl with ice and water. Decrease the heat under the saucepan to medium so the water is slowly simmering. Carefully add the eggs and cook for 12 minutes, then place them in the ice bath for 10 minutes. This will prevent the eggs from cooking any further and allow them to cool slightly so they are easy to peel.

Peel the eggs, cut them in half, and remove the yolks. Set aside. Roughly chop the egg whites and set aside.

In a bowl, combine the egg yolks, mayonnaise, mustard, lemon juice, olive oil, and salt and pepper. Mash together with a fork until you have a smooth and creamy consistency. Place the egg whites in the bowl and gently fold them in with a spoon.

Serve the egg salad on the toast. If desired, top with avocado slices and snipped chives.

SERVES 4

I cannot resist a soup that contains eggs. There is something extremely satisfying about cracking an egg, dropping it into a hot broth, and watching it puff up and solidify as it quickly cooks. As my daughter would say, "The eggs look like little clouds," as they have a beautiful light and airy texture when cooked this way. This is one of those meals that I turn to when I don't feel like cooking or have an unstocked fridge.

Italian egg drop soup (stracciatella)

In a large pot, bring the chicken stock to a boil over high heat. Add the pastina and cook for 3–4 minutes, until the pastina is al dente.

While the pastina cooks, in a bowl, whisk together the eggs, parmesan, semolina flour, parsley, and nutmeg (if using). Season with salt and pepper.

Decrease the heat to low and slowly pour the egg mixture into the soup. Gently stir once with a wooden spoon and then let sit without stirring while the eggs get fluffy and set. They will float on top of the broth. Gently stir, breaking up the eggs. Stir in the lemon zest (if using).

Ladle the soup into individual bowls and serve with a sprinkling of parmesan and parsley (if using).

SERVES 4

1 quart (1 liter) chicken stock

½ cup (100 g) pastina (soup pasta)

4 eggs

½ cup (50 g) grated parmesan, plus more for serving

1 tablespoon semolina flour

1 cup (20 g) flat-leaf parsley leaves, finely chopped, plus more (optional) for serving

¼ teaspoon ground nutmeg (optional)

Sea salt

Freshly ground black pepper

1 teaspoon grated lemon zest (optional)

During COVID, I was determined to master the art of pasta making. Using my $5 pasta machine that I found at the thrift store, I practiced how to make pasta almost every day by studying every pasta book I could get my hands on and taking online pasta classes hosted by my friend Meryl from Pasta Social Club. I am happy to report that I now make pasta like an Italian nonna and once you learn, too, you'll never go back to box pasta!

Egg pasta dough

In a large bowl, combine the flour, semolina, and salt. Transfer the mixture to a pasta board or clean work surface. Make a well in the center of the flour that is deep and wide enough to hold the eggs.

Place the whole eggs and egg yolks in the middle of the flour well and whisk together with a fork. While you're whisking, slowly bring in the flour from the edges of the well and whisk it into the eggs until a thick, custard-like paste forms. When you can no longer whisk the flour and egg with a fork, bring the flour from the edges into the well with your hands or a dough scraper and begin to knead the dough into a ball.

Knead the dough for 10 minutes, or until a firm, smooth dough ball forms that is moist and not sticky. Every dough is different so you will need to go by feel. If your pasta dough is too wet, very gradually add small amounts of flour. If it's too dry, lightly wet your hands and continue to knead it.

Place the dough in a bowl and cover well with plastic wrap or a clean, damp kitchen towel. Let rest for a minimum of 30 minutes.

Uncover the dough and cut it into quarters. Take one-quarter of the dough and cover the remainder so it does not dry out.

Place the dough on a lightly floured pasta board or work surface. Roll the dough out with a rolling pin into a rectangular shape that is ⅛ inch (3 mm) thick. Roll the dough through a pasta machine on the widest setting (number 7 on my pasta machine). Fold the dough in half, then flatten with a rolling pin. Turn the dough 90 degrees and roll it back through the machine. Repeat.

Roll the dough through a narrower setting (number 4 or 5 on my pasta machine) and fold the dough in half. Repeat this step twice.

Finally, roll the dough on the second-narrowest setting (number 2 on my pasta machine), until you have a long rectangular pasta sheet that is roughly 4 inches (10 cm) wide and paper-thin. Dust the pasta sheet with flour, lay it on a floured surface, and let the dough slightly cure (dry out) for 5–10 minutes. Repeat with the remaining dough.

SERVES 4–6

ALSO USED IN:

Garlic confit ragu bolognese 39

Pasta alla vodka 100

400 g (3½ cups) tipo "00" flour, plus more for dusting

⅓ cup (50 g) semolina flour, plus more for dusting

1 teaspoon sea salt

200 g whole eggs (about 4)

50 g egg yolks (about 3)

TIP

When kneading your pasta dough, think of it as a wave. When you push the dough away from you, the wave is going back out to the ocean. When you pull the dough toward you, you are riding the wave back to the shore.

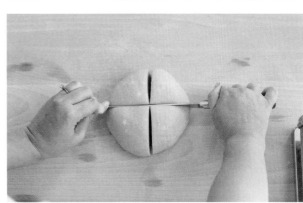

TO MAKE TAGLIATELLE

Lightly flour a pasta sheet, then gently fold it in half. Continue to fold the dough in half until you can't fold it anymore. Using a knife, cut the sheet into ribbons roughly ¼ inch (8 mm) wide. Unravel the pasta ribbons. Curl the pasta into a nest and dust with semolina flour.

Fresh tagliatelle is perfect for my Garlic Confit Ragu Bolognese (page 39).

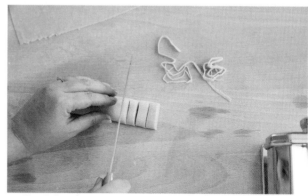

TO MAKE FARFALLE

Lightly flour a pasta sheet. Using a sharp knife or fluted pasta cutter, cut the pasta sheet into a grid of 1½ × 1¼-inch (4 × 3 cm) rectangles. Place a rectangle with one of the longer sides facing you. Position your thumb at the base of the rectangle, your index finger in the middle, and your middle finger at the top.

Now bring your fingers and thumb together, squeezing the rectangle in the center to form a bow tie shape. Fluff out the edges. Repeat with the remaining dough, then let dry for 15 minutes before cooking.

Fresh farfalle is perfect for my Pasta alla Vodka (page 100).

Acknowledgments

Thank you to Simon Element for taking a chance with a first-time Australian cookbook author! I still pinch myself that my book will be on American store shelves. A huge thank-you to my editors Katie McClimon and Doris Cooper. You made the process of writing a cookbook extremely seamless and enjoyable. You were also so patient with me while I navigated life and work with a newborn and toddler. Thank you to everyone who worked on this book on the Simon Element team: Richard Rhorer, Kristina Juodenas, Jen Wang, Laura Jarrett, Jessie McNiel, Alyssa diPierro, Grace Noglows, and Jessica Preeg.

Thank you to my Australian publisher, Plum, for taking a chance with a first-time author and making my dream of writing a cookbook come true. A special thank you to my publisher, Mary Small, who spent countless hours over coffee with me discussing the direction and vision for this book. I always left our meetings feeling so inspired and ready to take on the world. Thank you to my project editor, Clare Marshall, who made the daunting task of writing a book a breeze. I have loved working with you both! Thank you to my incredibly talented creative team for making this book more beautiful than I ever could have imagined. Armelle Habib, who captured my food in the most stunning way and inspired me every day on set as a fellow food photographer. Karina Duncan, who beautifully styled every shot and brought my food to life. Andy Warren, who has designed this book in a way that looks and feels like an extension of my personality. Ariana Klepac, who edited this book with so much warmth and patience. I would always have a little smile on my face when I saw Ariana's emails pop up in my inbox. Thank you to the chefs on set, Meryl Batlle and Jonte Carlson. It was a joy to watch you both in the kitchen and have someone cook for me! I loved seeing how you applied your wealth of food knowledge to my recipes. You both taught me so much.

Thank you to Ash Bros Food Services for supplying us with the freshest and tastiest seafood. And thank you to Rich Glen Olive Oil. It will come as no surprise that we needed a lot of olive oil to create this book, and I am very grateful to Rich Glen, who supplied bottles and bottles of their beautiful olive oil for us. Thank you to Elliot at Pompello in Seddon, who is always able to find me the most gorgeous garlic! Thanks to Effie and Alanna at The Happy Apple, who always greet me with a smile and questions about what I am making for the day. I love my little community in Melbourne! You always brighten my day.

To my amazing management team, One Management, thank you for everything that you do! You work so hard and go above and beyond for me.

To my beautiful family: Joel, you are the most supportive, caring, and selfless partner. You have been my biggest advocate since day one and I appreciate everything that you do for me. I love you so much. To my mum, who is one of the strongest women I know and inspires me every day. Without your love for cooking, I would not be here writing this book. Thank you for teaching me everything you know about food and cooking, and for passing your passion onto me. To Joel's family, you are some of my biggest supporters, and I am so lucky to have you all in my life.

To my daughters, Indigo and Margot, I love you with all my heart and can't wait for you to treasure this book when you are older. I love watching you grow into smart, funny, fearlessly independent, and beautiful girls.

Last but not least, to my online audience. I wouldn't be where I am without you and I am so grateful to each and every one of you! You allow me to live out my dream every single day. A big special thank you to my US audience, who happens to be my largest. Thank you for helping bring this book to the States!

From one garlic girl to another, thank you!

Index

SIMON
ELEMENT

An Imprint of Simon & Schuster, LLC
1230 Avenue of the Americas
New York, NY 10020

First Simon Element hardcover edition June 2025

SIMON ELEMENT is a trademark of Simon & Schuster, LLC

For information about special discounts for bulk purchases,
please contact Simon & Schuster Special Sales at 1-866-506-1949 or
business@simonandschuster.com.

The Simon & Schuster Speakers Bureau can bring authors to your
live event. For more information or to book an event, contact the
Simon & Schuster Speakers Bureau at 1-866-248-3049 or visit our
website at www.simonspeakers.com.

Manufactured in China

10 9 8 7 6 5 4 3 2 1

Library of Congress Cataloging-in-Publication Data has been applied for.

ISBN 978-1-6680-7496-1
ISBN 978-1-6680-7497-8 (ebook)